THE ELIJAH YEARS

Insights for the `90s:
A Decade of Prophetic Restoration

By

Marc A. Dupont

For further information write:

Mantle of Praise Ministries, Inc.
15 Phelps Drive
Brampton, Ontario Canada L6X 3V8
FAX (905) 459-1094

Printed and Published in North America.

Note: All Scripture quotations are taken from the New American Standard Version of the Bible, except as otherwise noted.

Dedication

This book is dedicated to the past and present board members of Mantle of Praise Ministries - men and women who have wholeheartedly loved, accepted, and greatly encouraged Kim and I. To Mark and Dave Hoffman who gave us much needed acceptance and friendship, and a spiritual home during our wilderness years. To Lloyd and Sheri Frazier who gave us much love and encouragement to press on. To Ron and Caroline Allen who have continually shared not only their wisdom, but more importantly, their hearts with us. To John and Carol Arnott who greatly encourage us by being both risk - takers for the Kingdom of God and wonderful messengers of God's grace and compassion to the body of Christ. Especially, I would like to thank John Ruttkay, who helped me keep my sanity during the '80s with his balanced discernment and a truly unique and vital sense of humor which helped keep things in perspective.

Most of all, I want to express my thanks to my wife Kim, a board member of Mantle of Praise, and my main encouragement for the last 13 years. During those times she has selflessly encouraged me to go forward, often when she has not really understood where we've been or where exactly we're going. She has been relentless in her encouragement to have faith and trust God not only during the easy times but especially the difficult times. She has always believed in certain gifts in me when they often seemed dubious at best to me. As Proverbs 18:22 states: I knew I was in God's favor when she came into my life.

Finally, I dedicate this to the King of Kings and Lord of Lords: Jesus Christ, the Lamb of God and the Lion of the tribe of Judah. Thank you, Jesus, that You not only desire to bring us truth and compassion, but that to top everything off, You desire to be my best friend! Thank You for these days, and that You saved the best for last. May Your glory cover the earth as the waters do, and even more so!

Acknowledgments

I would wholeheartedly like to thank Mike Wourms and Kathryn Belsey for first of all editing this grammatical mess and making it presentable. Thank you, Mike, not only for your professionalism, but your encouragement and being willing to work with my crazy schedule.

CONTENTS

Introduction

This book was never intended from the beginning. It is comprised of the first 9 or so newsletters written by me and sent out to some 300 leaders around the world. The purpose was not to try to come up with a book, but to help keep churches and leaders informed about what Mantle of Praise was involved with, and what I was currently focused on in my preaching.

As the early and mid '90s progressed, I realized that these letters were at least partially chronicling the core message of what I believed the Holy Spirit was wanting to say in those seasons to part of the body of Christ. Not wanting to be presumptuous, I realize that it takes many unique people with many unique God-given perspectives to relate the whole of what the Holy Spirit may be wanting to say at any given season. At the same time, however, churches of many different denominations that I have had the privilege of being involved with have, at least to my face, expressed appreciation and gratitude for what little part of the overall perspective I have been able to share.

It is my hopes that anyone who reads this would find a little bit of help in understanding some of the hopes and visions that the Lord Jesus may have been breathing on their own spirits during a crucial time of God "turning the tables" on our Church order so that we might become more a house of prayer and less a well-managed religious program. It is also my hope that no one would read this and allow these words to direct their ministries. New Testament prophecy is to encourage, build up, to edify - not to control, condemn or manipulate! The gift of life through Jesus Christ means, among other things, that as sons and daughters and fellow heirs we can all seek God and be led by His wonderful Spirit.

Two notes of apology: One: these letters were originally written for pastors and church leaders who have, or should have, a good, healthy knowledge of the Bible. For some readers, you might find yourself having to jump around in your Bible as you read some of the chapters because I have used many biblical passages to illustrate the things I believed the Lord was giving me to say. My average reader consisted of pastors and leaders who desired, and still do, to be both led by the Spirit and to understand theologically why God is saying and doing the things He is doing. So, if you find yourself doing a lot of Bible page turning, I apologize, but it is always of great benefit to understand more of the Scriptures anyway.

Two: I am painfully aware that in my past letters there is a great deal of what can be called "prophetic pontificating". That is, heavy statements were made in such a way that it seems I am writing down or being condescending. That was not and is not my intent!

Thanks to John Sanford who helped me to realize that there is a great deal of difference between preaching to a live group and writing a letter to an intelligent, God-seeking individual. I would have edited all of that out, but then, the book would not have been true to what it really is: the first nine newsletters covering what I believe the Holy Spirit was giving me to say. And that is not to say that the Holy Spirit wants anyone to speak down to another. It is just that this is very much a collection of letters that are definitely dated.

If anyone is offended by some of those "pontificating" lines, I truly apologize. As stated earlier, New Testament prophetic ministry is not to control, manipulate, or condemn, but to encourage and exhort.

Habakuk 2:3: *"For the revelation awaits an appointed time; it speaks of the end and will not prove false. Though it linger, wait for it; it will certainly come and will not delay."*

Chapter One

The First Celebration of the Nineties

At present, the Lord is seeing one crucial division occur among His people. It is not a division of doctrine about the Holy Spirit or eschatology, although we have certainly used these to create problems. Rather, it is a separation between those who are turning their hearts to the Lord and those who relish religion more than relationship.

Malachi, in prophesying about John the Baptist, says that in the spirit of Elijah, God will restore the hearts of the children to the fathers and the fathers to the children. During their ministries, both Elijah and John the Baptist had hard words for Israel. They spoke about the sovereignty of God over His children. The critical point of success for each of them in serving God was seeing the people of God, in their hearts, come to a place of repentance. To be more precise, they aimed to see people begin to understand the Lord's complete sovereignty and to humbly yield to His revealed glory and absolute holiness.

Not coincidentally, the primary focus in the nineties among many churches and denominations has been on intimacy with the Lord. Different labels and semantics are being used, but the bottom line is the Spirit of God is drawing the hearts of the children of God to the Father. The teachings range from holiness to prayer, repentance, prophecy, etc., but people are beginning to hunger for more than just knowing they are going to heaven; they also crave the *"spirit of wisdom and revelation"* (Ephesians 1:17, NAS) in the knowledge of the Father.

Malachi states that on the day the Lord of Hosts prepares His own possession, He will spare those who serve Him as sons (Malachi 3:17). Internationally, much is happening now with the kingdom of God compared to the prior decade. Even groups denying God speaks today believe we are in a special time frame. We are not just near the time of the Lord's return, but we are actually in the betrothal period spoken about in Hosea (Hosea 2:14).

This is a time God has allowed His people to wander in the wilderness. Our pride, complacency, and unbelief that God can do something so much bigger than we have yet seen could keep us in that wilderness, unless we are renewed through intimacy with our Lord.

The good part of Hosea's story was when Gomer fell into her old sins, God sent Hosea into the wilderness to find her again and to speak words of kindness to her. Then came a restoration complete with mercy, compassion, and provision.

The last fifteen years have seen an exodus from the Church. The phenomenon of confused and frustrated church members has touched almost every part of the body of Christ. Many church leaders during these years began to wonder if perhaps they were missing something, while others searched out new methods of church growth in an effort to stay current.

Often such leadership uncertainty has resulted in "train jumping." This is when a pastor or congregation suddenly changes programs or goals and attempts to duplicate the newest movement, but instead only succeeds in derailing the church and losing many members.

Other times, leaders have looked at church unrest and discerned it as rebellion, immaturity, emotionalism, or lack of faith. In light of this, it is important to remember that Jesus Himself, using a whip, drove the sheep and oxen out of the Temple. His disciples remembered later that it was written, *"Zeal for your house will consume me" (John 2:17; NIV).*

Jesus was not interested in people relating to the Father through a system. He wanted people who were zealous for God. If He had not driven those sheep from the Temple, they would have been sold for slaughter by a corrupt religious system. The same can hold true today for pastors with "sheep" and "oxen" in their care.

Vision

Proverbs says when there is no vision or revelation the people are unrestrained (Proverb 29:18; NAS). Certainly the Western Church in modern times seems to be without restraint.

Whether you look at liberal interpretations, the quantity of blatant sin, or lack of unity in the Church, today's times are similar to when Israel had no king (Judges 17:6). For instance, the Bible says when there was no king everyone did what was right in his own eyes. And, again, when people were going out to the wilderness to hear John the Baptist (remember, Malachi referred to him as the spirit of Elijah), the message was given: *"Repent, for the kingdom of heaven is near"* (Matthew 3:2, NIV).

When the people of Elijah's time went to Mount Carmel, they repented of following false gods; then they declared, *"the Lord He is God, the Lord He is God"* (I Kings 18:39, NIV). They had come into a deeper revelation that the Lord is not just the savior or comforter, but He is God almighty and as such is king over everything.

Interestingly, the very name of Elijah means "the Lord is God." This is the essence of John's message: proclaiming the complete kingship of God over His people. But to get that revelation, with both Elijah and John, people had to go into the wilderness.

11

So how are we to think about vision? How are we to determine specific direction for our lives, especially now that so much is happening with the kingdom of God?

Unfortunately, there has been a confusion of priorities. We have talked and taught that vision, or prophetic direction, is primarily for ministry or outward activity. Obviously, the Lord desires to give vision for extending His kingdom, but it is not the chief purpose of the Lord's desiring to communicate with us.

When we as human parents rejoice because our children are born with healthy eyes and ears, it is not so they can go out and make some money or enter the family business. We are glad because our children will be able to learn to communicate with us. And it is a great day when a child can verbally identify us as its mother or father.

For the same reason we rejoice over our children's development, the Father desires His children to have eyes to see and ears to hear - so we might know Him and, as good children, learn to imitate Him.

Jesus said He could do nothing on His own initiative, but He only did what He saw the Father doing (John 5:19-20). Paul prayed for the church at Ephesus, that the Father would give it a spirit of wisdom and revelation in the knowledge of Himself. Paul continued in his prayer, that the eyes of the Ephesians' hearts would be enlightened to know the riches of their inheritance (Ephesians 1:17-18).

What inheritance? The inheritance that they now had as sons of the living God. In Romans, Paul says the sons of God are led by the Spirit of God, and we have received a spirit of adoption or sonship. Therefore, we may freely cry out "Abba" or "Papa" (Romans 8:14-15).

When Jesus addresses the lukewarm church at Laodicea (which is symbolic the Church today), He promises to give it gold refined by fire. This brings us back to Malachi. When Malachi prophesies of the time of John the Baptist, he begins by speaking of a period of undergoing the "refiners fire." It is to be a time of purifying when no one is able to stand (Malachi 3:2).

This is the fire Jesus advises the church of Laodicea to buy. Jesus quotes the prophet Isaiah, who says to the people of His time, *"Ever hearing but never understanding...ever seeing but never perceiving. For this people's heart has become calloused"* (Matthew 13:14-15; NIV).

The NIV translation uses the word "calloused." Certainly, the Church of the Western world today is a calloused Church. Not only are we often lacking in compassion and real love, but our motivations seem to come more from the world's value system than from the kingdom of God. Jesus said not to be like the people of the world who seek first after money and materialism.

Why, then, is there so much teaching on prayer that is focused on getting a hold of the goods of this world? Instead, Jesus says our Father knows we have need of such things, but we must seek first the King and His rule.

The word "calloused," according to Webster's Dictionary, means "hardened and thick-skinned." This works both ways - not only are we in the Church often insensitive to the needs of those around us, but we tend to be hard of hearing when it comes to the Holy Spirit. Some would say, "The gifts are working so we must be hearing from the Holy Spirit," but Jesus said there would be those who would prophecy, cast out demons, and heal the sick in His Name but He would not know them.

It is also not enough to have a good Bible knowledge or theology. Jesus said to some of the leaders of His time, *"You search the scriptures because you think that in them you have eternal life; and it is these that bear witness of me"* (John 5:39, NAS). It is also possible to have a good testimony and still miss out. For example, in the parable of the ten virgins five were locked outside the wedding party, not because they had lost their testimony but because they did not really know the bridegroom.

Joel 2:28 makes two basic observations about the end-time outpouring of the Holy Spirit:

First, the Lord will reach out to all of mankind. Undoubtedly, we are in a time frame today when that is beginning to happen. For from the Amazon Basin to the unreached peoples of the Soviet Union, the kingdom of God is spreading across the globe at an unprecedented rate. Even among Muslim peoples in Africa, conversions to Christ and signs and wonders have dramatically increased.

Second, the people of God during these times will be people who have eyes to see and ears to hear. I believe Joel speaks of a people who, rather than solely experiencing Pentecostal or Charismatic phenomena, will be like Jesus and attempt to do the things they see the Father doing.

The last two generations in the Western world have seen a radical breakdown of the family unit. One of the chief problems has been a loss of true father figures. Too many times the fathers' love is not rooted in commitment and intimacy with the children. In addition, the authority level usually is either non-existent or abusive. This syndrome has naturally led children to rebellion and confusion concerning identity and values.

This state of problems has also affected church structure and leadership. Many Christians, while clinging to their salvation and Christian ethics, have a very real problem with spiritual authority in their lives. The situation is often compounded by leaders in a church also having deep-rooted problems with authority in their lives. This results in leaders who, because of personal insecurity, compensate by heavy-handed control.

The worst symptom of the overall problem is that Father God, the very throne and authority of everything, is ignored and the Church too much resembles a system rather than a people who know and are led by the Spirit.

The last few years have seen the beginning of the things Malachi spoke of, at least symbolically. There has been, for many leaders, a real desire to learn to commune with the Father. Many are agreeing with Jeremiah 7:11 (NAS): we have made the Church into a self-centered and self-promoting system; instead, it should be a "house of prayer" (Isaiah 56:7, NAS).

As many in leadership reach out to know the Father, the Father is revealing His holiness more clearly. This revelation brings about insight into our hearts and motives, so we may see things as the Father sees them.

To lead us to another revelation of God's sight, 1 Kings 8:38 says when we pray we should individually be aware of the afflictions of our own hearts and spread our hands towards the Temple. This reaching for the Temple symbolizes coming with honesty before the throne of the Father. From such a posture, we develop humility. In the end, God is pleased, for Isaiah says the Lord does not look on the proud but on the broken and humble (Isaiah 66:1-2).

The Prodigal Son

The Holy Spirit teaches us how to seek first the kingdom of God in our hearts. The fruit of that is (agreeing with the elders in the book of Revelation) learning how to throw down our crowns, egos, and ambitions before the throne of God and worship Him with a renewed sense of His glory and holiness.

We can only achieve this sense of His true nature when our gifts and ministries are renewed by the refiner's fire. We know they need refining because our abuse of gifts in the world is wasteful, and our abuse of spiritual gifts is sinful. In fact, many are learning from the Holy Spirit that even though good things may have been happening in our ministries, in the name of Jesus, we have not necessarily been doing those things out of pure hearts.

The refiner's fire of Malachi 3 that purifies our hearts, or buying gold like the Church of Laodicea (Revelation 3), is not an easy or light thing - it costs everything. Consequently, we find it difficult to die to self. The end result for many as they come to the Father is they settle into a slave's attitude: "Now all I want is to be a slave to you, God, and receive a slave's portion."

That is how radical the Holy Spirit's revelation is. It is a revelation of the Father and His throne which makes the value of everything else, especially personal glory, fade away.

The good news is that traditionally this is exactly how the Lord works. Indeed, the most basic of all patterns with the Lord is when we repent He always responds with mercy and grace. As we begin to identify with the prodigal son, the Father is free to draw us in as sons.

This is a time of incredible celebration for many who have been truly seeking the Father. It will be a celebration ordained by God and anointed by His Spirit. In such a season of homecoming, the Father will bestow five distinct blessings on His prodigal children.

First, He will fold us in an embrace and a kiss. The embrace symbolizes complete acceptance into the household as a son. The kiss symbolizes the Father's desire for us to intimately know His love.

Second, He will cover us with a robe. More than ever, many will find in this season they have a greater covering and protection over their lives in the areas of temptation and spiritual warfare.

Third, He will give the ring, which signifies greater power and authority in prayer and ministry. We will experience that power and authority when we comprehend what Jesus means here, "Pray to the Father, in My Name". He never meant this as a formula but for us to understand we should learn to communicate with the Father. He desires that we know His voice and also that to pray in Jesus' name means our hearts should be motivated like His - to want to please the Father, no matter what the cost.

Fourth, He shods our feet with sandals. Sandals, shoes, or the feet are quite often Bible symbols of the gospel or being a messenger of the good news. In this time of homecoming, many Christians will be wearing their good news sandals and see the kingdom grow in people who were previously far from the Lord. Not that everybody will be an evangelist, but there will be a greater freedom to communicate the Lord to people as we ourselves learn to trust and submit on a deeper level. As a result, many churches will experience "end-time fruit" in their ministries. They will begin to sample the end time moving of the Holy Spirit in a sovereign way.

Also, I believe there will be a great move towards unity in the body of Christ as we begin to realize the Father's guideline - *"Perfect love casts out fear"* (I John 4:18, NAS).

Last, the fattened calf symbolizes the party the Lord wants us to experience. For many of us, it seems hard this day and age to relate to the joy of the Lord. It is difficult to be happy during grim years, but in this season, the Father is going to celebrate the "homecoming" of many of His sons who have been out doing their own things.

One pastor of a mid-size church fits the picture of what I have been describing here. The Lord had allowed the church and him to go through a death process over a couple of years, even as they earnestly sought after the Father. At the end of the two years, I visited this church's seminar: "What the Father is saying."

On the last day of the seminar, the Lord had me prophesy the following over the pastor:

Now the Lord is welcoming you home as the prodigal son. This is a year of new acceptance from the Father. The worldly rebellion you brought into your life with God is now broken. You and those around you, the Church, are going to have a special year of celebration and harvest.

On the following Monday, the pastor contacted me and related that on Sunday the Holy Spirit had come over the Church in a radical way. He said he had never seen such a powerful freedom for worship and celebration before.

When he told me this over the phone, the Lord spoke to me and said this was the Father's homecoming party for that church and that the fattened calf was being prepared.

In a unique way, this story is an example for the larger Church. The Father is really drawing the hearts of His children to Himself. The Lord, along with the multitude of angels, is joyfully preparing a party for the children responding to His invitation. He is preparing for the great harvest to come.

Chapter Two

Mounting Up With Wings of Eagles

Intimacy with God is the challenge facing the Church today. Isaiah 40:31 (NAS) powerfully speaks about the strength a close relationship with the Lord brings: *"Those who wait on the Lord will gain new strength; they will mount up with wings like eagles, they will run and not get tired, they will walk and not become weary."*

Of course, Isaiah is making an analogy here, but, nonetheless, he is speaking about the possibility of a fuller experience of knowing and serving God. In general, when we look at the evangelical Church today, we see few people who continue to walk and not grow weary, let alone many whose lifestyles reflect knowing and experiencing the fullness of the Spirit.

Isaiah, when prophesying that the Holy Spirit's fullness would be on Jesus, said Jesus would wear a "mantle of praise" instead of a "spirit of fainting" (Isaiah 61:3, NAS). Regrettably, the Western Church tends to be dressed in the latter.

This is reflected in the quantity of "quick-fix" books in Christian bookstores. These books somehow impart head knowledge of the fruit of the Spirit, but they do so without taking people through the experience of walking and being filled with the Spirit. As a result, readers fail to be challenged to obey what the Lord is saying on a personal level.

What the Lord is saying at the close of this century ought to serve as a radical wake-up call. The Church would no doubt respond but for a tremendous paradox facing it: wholesale pride, complacency, and weakness are rampant in the Church; meanwhile, God's call has been placed on the Church to demonstrate His kingdom.

Coming into the last days - when the Spirit of God will rest on young, old, rich, and poor, when young men will prophesy, old ones dream dreams, and men and women see visions (Joel 2:28) - we are a people who have that spirit of fainting. Instead of changing from glory to glory, we are often a people who go from frustration to frustration, our lives governed more by trials than by the Spirit of the Lord God.

Discerning the Signs of the Times

The disciples, whether they were cognizant of it or not, were caught up in a time frame pivotal for all humanity. Jesus said to them, *"Many prophets and righteous men longed to see what you see but did not see it, and to hear what you hear and did not hear it"* (Luke 10:24, NAS). The ways in which Jesus, the Messiah, moved throughout Israel were so revolutionary, not even the religious leaders, who should have known what was happening, were prepared for Him.

This radicalness of Jesus was not a religious fanaticism or a legalistic austerity, but a complete demonstration of two things: the authority of the kingdom of God, and the heart of the Father. For that reason Jesus said to Philip that if Philip had seen Jesus he had seen the Father.

Coming into the present, we also live in a time frame that, while it is not the pivotal time of the cross and resurrection, is, in fact, a historical time, a time when the Spirit of God is moving on humanity like never before. It has been said there have been more people coming to Jesus as Lord and being filled with His Spirit in the last twenty years than in the previous two thousand.

In the early `90s, the pace of the kingdom quickened. Many nations which have not had the gospel move in decades or centuries are now opening up, especially in the Muslim and third-world nations. When we look at things Jesus spoke of in Matthew 24, pertaining to the last days, such as wars, rumors of wars, earthquakes, famines, and droughts, it is highly possible that either we are in the last days or coming into them very quickly.

One has only to take a cursory look around the world to see this. For example, catastrophic events are commonplace in Sudan and other parts of Africa where millions and millions of people starve daily. In Mozambique, one out of every three children never lives to its fifth birthday. In Bangladesh, in 1991, over 140,000 people died from flooding and a cyclone. The same year in Red China, there were millions homeless due to flooding that touched half the nation.

It is very easy to look at these tragedies, as well as the increase of hatred, sin, and violence in the world, and out of a motivation of fear, pray for the return of the Lord. This was the case during the 60's and 70's when many ministries looked at the culture and said the Lord's return was imminent.

However, significant world events occurred in the ensuing decades, demonstrating God's mercy in tarrying. For instance, if Jesus had come before 1990's, the Soviet Union, a nation of more than 290 million people, would never have experienced the incredible move of the gospel which is now being birthed all across that nation.

Again, God's mercy has been shown to Mozambique, which had had Marxist rule for over twenty years - complete with corruption, starvation, poverty, and persecution of Christianity. Today, the nation enjoys new freedoms, and the gospel is moving incredibly.

Jesus, in Matthew 24:8, said when these signs would take place they would be birth pangs of what is to come. Just as final labor pains for a pregnant woman are incredibly difficult to bear, the time comes when the baby emerges and the pain is forgotten over the joy of the child. Jesus said during this time the gospel would be preached in all nations.

It is this time frame I believe we are witnessing - a time when Joel says the Spirit of God will touch all mankind. Joel prophesies of a time when - just as the kingdom cut like a knife through Israel with Jesus - the kingdom of God today, by the sword of the Spirit, shall cut through the whole world.

Who are the people who are going to wield that Sword? It is going to be the young, the old, male and female, rich and poor. It is going to be the people who have eyes to see and ears to hear. It is going to be the people of whom Jesus spoke, who know Him not just as Savior, but as the Lord God almighty.

That is, the people who are going to be effective for God are people who know in their hearts - not just their heads - that Jesus is in the Father and the Father is in Jesus. People who in their attitudes and practices relate to life as though they were representatives not just of free fire insurance but representatives of the King of the universe.

This is the King who says, *"All authority has been given to Me in Heaven and on earth."* The people who follow such a king are going to be the peacemakers in the huge harvest to come. They are going to be the ones who, because of intimacy with the Father, are led by His Holy Spirit.

These are going to be the ones both Jesus and Paul say are going to be known as the Sons of God. These ones will do the things Jesus did.

These are going to be the people whom Joel prophesies will see visions, dream dreams, and themselves prophesy. Because they are filled with the Father's love which casts out fear, these will be the ones free to touch the world's cultures with the prophetic sword of the Spirit.

The Battle Call is Sounding, but Where are the Soldiers?

It is too easy in the Western Church today to be overfed, weak, and complacent. We often resemble spiritual couch-potatoes, constantly entertained by vicarious Christianity. We can glibly sing "Onward Christian Soldier" in our services, with false concepts of what it means to preach the gospel. To spit out doctrinally correct rhetoric is not the same as ministering to people.

Not only have we failed with the gospel to have an overwhelming impact on the cultures of the last two generations, but even most church people are unable to relate to the world. We have become like the religious leaders to whom Jesus said, *"Go and learn what this means: I desire compassion, and not sacrifice"* (Matthew 9:13, NAS).

Those leaders spent hours and hours every day studying the word of God, but they were without a clue as to the heart of the Father. In like manner, we are the last days' church of Laodicea (Revelation 3:14). We think we are wealthy and have need of nothing, yet we do not understand we are wretched, poor, blind, and naked.

The prophet Jeremiah asks the men of Judah, *"If you have run with the footmen, and they have tired you out, then how can you compete with horses? If you fall down in a land of peace, How will you do in the thicket of the Jordan?"* (Jeremiah 12:5, NAS).

This is a valid question for today. Jesus says in the last days - during the time the gospel will be preached to all nations - there will be tremendous demonic warfare against the people of God:

23

*Then you will be handed over to be
persecuted and put to death, and you will
be hated by all nations because of me. At
that time many will turn away from the faith
and will betray and hate each other, and
many false prophets will appear and
deceive many people. Because of the
increase of wickedness, the love of most
will grow cold, but he who stands firm to the
end will be saved. (Matthew 24:9-13)*

We are at a time when both demonic warfare and
the pace of what God is doing and saying are increasing
dramatically. Already, because of pride and
complacency, many ministries, which in recent years
were on the cutting edge of God's activity, are no longer
current. For many Christians who are not catching what
the Spirit is saying, it will be increasingly harder to catch
up.

Jesus says, *"I am the gate; whoever enters through
Me will be saved."* But that is only half the verse. He
continues, *"and will come in and go out, and find
pasture"* (John 10:0, NIV). This is hard for many people
to relate to. What does Jesus mean "go in and out?" In
and out of what? Is not the pasture in the sheep pen?

Of the first generation out of Egypt, only Joshua and
Caleb entered into the promised land, because they
were the ones who believed God could deal with the
giants of the land. At a relatively advanced age, Caleb
said he was still strong for going out and doing war and
coming in. When Caleb, at age eighty-five, went out, he
went to do warfare against the enemies of God. He
went out and captured more territory for Israel. When
Jesus ministered to the woman at the well, His disciples
were amazed He would even talk to a Samaritan
woman. A good and proper Jewish man would not do

that.   When they told Jesus they had food for the evening, Jesus replied, *"I have food to eat that you know nothing about"* (John 4:32, NIV)

Too much of the Church today is like the disciples in that situation. The real food God has for us is learning how to give, instead of constantly taking and taking. We think the good grass is in the Church. But the harvest is outside, and the Lord is calling us to be like Caleb, to go out and do warfare on behalf of the kingdom of God.

What are we Living For?

Bob Dylan's song in the late '70s, *Serve Somebody*, relates that there is no middle ground: either a person will end up serving God or someone else. That is how it is in the Kingdom of God, especially in the last days race of running with the Holy Spirit. But often, when it comes to stepping out in faith, we resemble Saul when Samuel was ready to crown him as king of Israel - he was hiding behind the baggage (I Samuel 10:22). In contrast, when the Lord was ready to raise up David, a man God said "had a heart for God," David did not even want to wear Saul's armor when facing the giant. All he wanted was the slingshot that he had grown up with, and a few rocks. David, because of his zealousness for God, was ready to go for it (I Samuel 17:37-40).

But, like Saul, we are often loaded down with so much baggage it becomes a trap for us, and keeps us from being able to respond when the Lord wants to anoint us. Paul writes to Timothy, *"Suffer hardship with me as a good soldier of Christ Jesus. No soldier in active service entangles himself in the affairs of everyday life, so that he may please the one who enlisted him as a soldier."* (II Tim. 2:3-4, NAS)

When Jesus, in Matthew 6, contrasts serving the world's spirit with serving the kingdom of God, he speaks about not getting caught up in the attitudes and priorities of world cultures. In the Western world today, everything possible and impossible is done in the continual quest to make life comfortable so that we might live a life of luxury. The hidden trap is that to obtain a Madison Avenue life, we become slaves to the system.

It is time for the body of Christ to lose weight. It is time to disentangle ourselves from all the unnecessary baggage the world tells us we need so we can run the race as if we want to win. This does not mean quitting jobs and neglecting responsibilities. But in the decision-making processes controlling our money and time the Lord desires more governance over our hearts and motives.

A change of jobs or a promotion with more money is not always from the Lord, especially if it is going to dominate more of your time. Having to have a new car or a bigger house is not always the necessity we think it is, especially if it is going to control our check books.

The Lord wants us to learn how to move in the Spirit. This involves more than going to Spirit-filled meetings. It also means being part of the move of God in setting the captives free and healing the broken hearts.

Ministering to others will teach that a lifestyle of giving ourselves to the world is better than a lifestyle of constantly focusing on our needs. For many this will mean doing things that, at this time, are not common in most churches.

One opportunity might be to go once or twice a month to poor areas and distribute food, share the gospel, and pray for the sick. Another might be to give up a yearly vacation - both time and money - to go on a three-week ministry trip to the Soviet Union or Nicaragua. For others, it might mean an opportunity to learn to live on God's economy - perhaps living on only 60% of annual income so that missionaries might be financially supported.

The possibilities are as endless as the uniqueness with which the Lord has created us. One thing is definite, it is time to get free. It is time to start spiritually jogging and exercising, because the Lord, in the outpouring of the Holy Spirit of which Joel speaks, is inviting us to be part of the greatest move of the Spirit the Church has ever experienced.

He is calling us to wait on Him, and to KNOW THAT HE IS GOD. He is calling us to walk and not faint, run and not be weary, and to mount up prophetically and see what the Spirit of the living God is doing.

In May, 1991, I met a man in Gothenburg, Sweden, who exemplified both sacrificing and creativity in the love of God. He had already achieved moderate success in the business world and knew his possibilities for a successful career in making money; however, he walked away from that for a mobile, street-side hot dog stand and began to sell hot dogs in the prostitution area of the city.

He purposely worked nights, when the most traffic of pros and street people flowed. Basically, he was doing on-the-job evangelism. He laid down a foundation of being open and friendly to the people on the streets, and relationships of trust began to happen.

Like Jesus, hanging with prostitutes, thieves, and tax gatherers, he was taking the reality of God's love to people who probably would never attend a church service. Because he had a hunger to evangelize and was also open to the leading of the Holy Spirit, this man was taking the gospel to a hidden people, a group untouched by the Church.

The Holiness of David

There has been criticism of this type of message, an argument that we cannot be super-spiritual people who are perfect. That is true enough, if we are speaking about legalistic perfection. But when we look at the history of God working with mankind, it is possible to have a Church that is hot rather than the lukewarm condition of Laodicea. The early Church lived in an expression of Christ that carried on the works of the Lord in touching the culture powerfully, rather than just drawing forth theological symbolism from the miracles Jesus did in the past.

The fourth chapter of the book of Acts gives this description of life in the early Church:

> *All the believers were one in heart and mind. No one claimed that any of his possessions was his own, but they shared everything they had. With great power the apostles continued to testify to the resurrection of the Lord Jesus, and much grace was upon them all. There were no needy persons among them. For from time to time those who owned lands or houses sold them, brought the money from the sales and put it at the apostles' feet, and it was distributed to anyone as he had need.* (Acts 4:32-35, NIV)

It should go without saying this is a far cry from the state of the Church today, especially in Western world countries. The example of sacrificial money giving is very crucial, because a person's use of money is one of the key indicators of where their heart, or their treasure, is. There is no mention in the book of Acts that the early Church lived in some sort of sinless perfection. They were not a church without problems but a church deeply caught up in a radical love affair with the Lord.

David, the first true king of Israel, was chosen by the Lord to replace Saul, the first actual king of Israel. He was preferred by the Lord not because of sinlessness;

on the contrary, David committed major sins, such as adultery, murder, and sometimes disobedience against the word of the Lord. But God chose David because he was a man after the Lord's heart (I Samuel 12:14).

The most important character trait about David was his love affair with the Lord. It was his treasure which neither moth nor rust could destroy and no thief could steal. Like challenging Goliath, his love affair was something worth dying for. It was a love affair of sometimes reckless abandonment.

At this time the Lord is wooing the Church, in preparation for the wedding to come. Revelation 19 says this:

> *Let us rejoice and be glad and give the glory to Him, for the marriage of the Lamb has come and His bride has made herself ready. And it was given to her to clothe herself in fine linen, bright and clean; for the fine linen is the righteous acts of the saints.*
> (Revelation 19:7-8, NAS)

It is time for the Church of Laodicea to go through the fire and clothe itself in the white garments the Lord has prepared for us (Revelation 3:18).

Chapter Three

Joshuas and Calebs for a Free Generation

If we think of revival not as artificial Church noise but as the Kingdom of God coming over cultural groups and nations, then we can think about it as a two-step process.

First, revival brings restoration to the Church. In fact, restoration is a more precise word to use than revival. Restoration means returning to its original state something of value which has become worn or blemished.

Second, restoration allows the outpouring of the Lord's compassion and reality on the general populace, through the people of God. When we look at the restoration Elijah brought, followed by the ministry of Elisha, we see this scriptural pattern. It is repeated with John the Baptist's ministry, followed by the coming of the Lamb of God. Both of these examples had a great affect on the societies of their day. Another poignant example is David, in Psalm 51, recognizing that the fruit of his own restoration to the presence of the Lord would be sinners being taught of the Lord.

Today we are in a similar prophetic period, when God is preparing His existing Church for a huge explosion of the gospel. In many areas of the world, the kingdom is tearing down walls of false gods. Part of being a prophetic church or person, however, is not merely hearing from the Father but being obedient and doing what He says.

Noah was not a prophet just because He knew what God was saying, he was a good prophet because he based his life, his hopes, and his dreams on preparing for what he believed God was going to do. As Church leaders today, it is not enough to be caught up in prophetic fervor, but we need to prepare for what God is going to do.

This means we not only have to recognize our need for being changed by God, but we must also realize this change is to free us to love the Father first, as Jesus did. Then we must do what Jesus did in preparation for returning to the Father.

Jesus' death on the cross did not bring us the message of the cross. No, for not only did Jesus give His life for us but He gathered, taught, and trained disciples to start and lead His Church after His return to the Father. Much of His time was spent strictly with His disciples, disciples the Father specifically gave Him. Most of the time Jesus was not teaching and healing the multitudes; rather, most of the time He shared His life, His soul, and His love of the Father with a small group of men, preparing them to be leaders of His future followers.

Our human nature dictates that bigger numbers mean more success. Jesus, when preparing His disciples, worked on the premise that quality is better than quantity.

Jesus deliberately said things like *"eating His body, and drinking His blood"*, knowing that not only would the crowds be confused by this but that many of His disciples would also leave Him, thinking Him insane. According to the Apostle John, Jesus even asked His closest friends and disciples if they were going to leave Him, too (John 6:67).

The point being was this: at that time the primary thing for Jesus to accomplish, other than the cross and resurrection, was to make disciples. But not just any disciples, for belief and obedience were not enough. He specifically prepared these twelve men to be the first apostles of His Church, which He knew was going to dramatically explode after Pentecost.

A Prophetic Generation to Kill Giants

As I stated in the previous chapter, the first generation out of Egypt never entered into the Promised Land. This was not because of Israel's sin with the Golden Calf but because of unbelief that God could take them into a land occupied by giants who were not only warriors but much more prepared for war then the Hebrew men were (Numbers 13).

When the people wanted to stone Joshua and Caleb for telling them to have faith in the Lord's goodness, God judged Israel and swore that none of their generation over twenty years of age, except Joshua and Caleb, would enter into the Promised Land. All of the others would die in the wilderness.

The writer of Hebrews says the people hardened their hearts when they heard the Lord speak (Hebrews 3:7-11). By so doing, they provoked the Lord to judgment. The children of that generation, however, did have faith to respond to the voice of the Lord.

What was the difference between the first and second generation? They had both seen the miracles, signs, and wonders, not only in Egypt but in escaping Pharaoh through the Red Sea. They had both experienced the manna and quail from above and water coming out of rocks.

The difference was this generation had grown up in freedom with God. As children, they had been used to seeing the Holy Spirit lead them, not only through Moses but being virtually tangible as a cloud of glory by day and fire by night.

As the Holy Spirit is being poured out today, especially on the children and those beginning to relate to God as a child, we are going to have a generation grow up. Not a generation of "church kids" but a generation experiencing the reality of a personal God who speaks and leads in a greater dimension than any previously.

Like the younger generation out of Egypt, this will be the generation to see the reality of what prophets like Joel and Habakkuk saw: the Spirit of God touching all mankind and the glory of God covering the earth as the waters do. This will be a generation which, because of its intimacy with the Lord, will have more faith in God to kill the demonic giants of the world's cultures than the Church today.

Many Christians have more faith in the antichrist's and Satan's ability to threaten the Church than they do in God's ability to touch the world in a powerful way.

Out of the Mouths of Babes and Infants

In recent years, often the strongest moving of the Holy Spirit I have seen has been with children under ten to twelve years of age. From Nigeria to Indiana, Toronto to Norway, the Holy Spirit is coming on kids today very freely and powerfully.

Not too long ago in Malmo, Sweden, while I was visiting a Christian School, the Holy Spirit began to fall on many of the students. There were a couple of twelve-year-old boys present who were not Christians. The Holy Spirit began to fill them as they opened up during the ministry time. I directed them to lay hands on one of their friends present also at the meeting and pray for Him in Jesus' name.

As they were praying for him, he fell to the floor and collapsed completely under the power of the Lord. The two boys who had not yet surrendered their lives were in total amazement. Like with Peter at Cornelius' house, the Holy Spirit wants to fill people who are crying out for the reality of God - He will even use young children!

Lately, during meetings where the Holy Spirit has been falling, many of the most creditable visions and prophesies I have heard have been out of the mouths of children.

In Hammar, Norway, September, 1991, a boy who was touched by the Holy Spirit was not experiencing any outward manifestations. But during the remainder of the day, he was unusually quiet and still. The next day he was back to his normal self. After dinner that evening, however, he said to his parents, "We need to pray more, we need to seek God together".

In Indiana, during a conference the previous year, we had a special prayer session for the children. We had prophecies for several kids around ten years of age that the Lord was going to use them prophetically. Imagine my delight when I found out from the Pastor that later that afternoon and evening one young boy in his congregation related several visions and words that He was receiving from the Holy Spirit.

These things happening with kids are not only important for their generation but they are symbolic for all of us. Malachi talks about how in the end times the hearts of the fathers will be restored to the children and the hearts of the children restored to the fathers. Well, right now our heavenly Father is bringing restoration to the heart of His children.

In the last days, if the Lord is going to break down the barriers of Islam, Hinduism, Buddhism, and Materialism, the movers of the kingdom will be those who - because they know the Father and know what the Father is saying and doing - are not led by either fear or circumstances. The Apostle Paul says, *"Those who are led by the Spirit of God are sons of God. For you did not receive a spirit that makes you a slave again to fear, but you received the Spirit of sonship. And by him we cry, "Abba, Father"* (Romans 8:14-15, NIV). These will be the peacemakers who will be called "the sons of God".

Father Figures for a Prophetic Church

As the body of Christ goes through the restoration years ahead and learns to be childlike, the Lord will establish father figures. Culturally, in North America and Europe, we are beginning to go into the third generation now where the family unit is almost non-existent. This is especially true of the young generation now, when more children are coming from broken families than intact ones.

Because of the growing rampage of divorce, child abuse, alcohol and drug-diseased parents, and parents unable to understand their responsibilities, I am calling the up-and-coming generation the "fatherless generation". Even for the two previous generations, too many families are actually dysfunctional, and children have grown up with warped perceptions of what it means to be parents. There is almost no understanding of what it means to set real example of selfless love for children. Despite this grim reality, our confidence does not have to be shaken by the advancing ruin; instead, it can powerfully rest in the Father, who is "a Father to the fatherless" (Psalm 68:5, NIV).

To a lesser degree, the same lack of selfless love has infiltrated the contemporary Church. There is no lack of gifted people in the Church today, but there is a definite lack of people prepared to give themselves to others as Jesus taught His disciples to do. As I Corinthians 4:14 (NIV) reads: *"You have ten thousand guardians in Christ, but you do not have many fathers"* ("but" is my addition). Many people in leadership have a passionate abandon in their hearts for the Lord, but, because they come from dysfunctional family situations, they cannot persevere in living out God's will for their lives.

It is not enough to say that we love God and are deeply committed to Him. John asks, "If we do not love the brother that we see, how can we love God whom we have not seen?" When asked the greatest commandment, Jesus did not just say the first, which is to love the Lord our God with all our hearts, but He continued by saying the second is almost the same in importance: to love our neighbor as ourselves (Mark 12:29-31). He demonstrated this by washing His disciples' feet, telling them if they wanted to be leaders like Him they were going to have to be involved in the lives (dirty feet) of His people.

This brings us to the point. Part of God's process in preparing the up-and-coming generation is to provide father figures. The problem is how can we be fathers if we have not learned first to be real brothers with one another? And how can we be real brothers with one another if we first have not learned how to be childlike with God the Father?

So in preparing the Church for an explosion of the Gospel, the Lord is making the foundation bigger and deeper. First, our relationship with the Father deepens in the intimacy discussed previously. Second, our understanding of what it means to have the Father's sacrificial love for people will broaden.

So what is a scriptural "father figure"? To the contemporary Church, with its strong values of theology and authority figures, we might say a father figure is someone in his fifties, or older, who is still in active leadership, and has been "successful" in pastoring or teaching.

But is that really all we need? If we look at the two older leaders of the Hebrews as they crossed over the Jordan, we see something a little more radical. If we looked only at Joshua's and Caleb's gifting or trained skills, we would get a methodological, patterned, or statistical type of sketch that might be interesting but would not really mean a thing.

The problem we have today in the Church is not so much a lack of gifting, but a lack of Godly character. Usually when we talk about "Godly character" in a person, we relate that to personal holiness, or a lifestyle filled with sacrifice. These things are certainly part of Godliness, but it is not a complete picture. The outstanding thing we see in both the lives of Joshua and Caleb is risk taking.

Currently, there is an established pattern today in leadership of once success happens (relating to money and numbers), complacency and safety become more valuable than new breakthroughs in the Kingdom. Even leaders who may have begun their ministries out of radical obedience to the Lord become entrenched in conservative, "don't-rock-the-boat" tradition. Often tradition comes out of past obedience and becomes our present bondage. Basically, once success is reached, often the risk taking stops.

God is an incredible risk taker, and when we cease to be risk takers we passively begin to settle into religious patterns rather than be led by the Spirit of God. Whether He was creating man in the Garden of Eden, giving His only begotten Son on the cross, or turning the leadership of the Church over to the twelve Apostles, God was and is an enormous risk taker.

I do not mean by "risk taker" someone who takes chances just for the sake of taking chances. What I am talking about is the difference between being religious and being spiritual. The prophet Samuel (I Samuel 15:22, NIV) said to Saul that God was not interested in his religious sacrifices. He said, *"To obey God is better than sacrifice"*. Jesus told the Scribes and Pharisees God was not interested in their sacrifices; instead, it was mercy He was after (Matthew 9:13). But the Scribes and Pharisees were too concerned about their reputations to take a risk and demonstrate God's mercy and compassion to prostitutes, thieves, and lowlife.

As time goes on, in the 90's and beyond, God is going to be calling church leaders to be taking more visible and costly risks. It is going to be more costly to be obedient to the Father in future years. Why? Because God is pulling out all the stops; His kingdom is on the move, and like Jesus approaching the cross, our crosses are going to get bigger.

The Lord is going to force leaders to deal with their motivations. Are we living for the kingdom of God or for the kingdom of man? Is our biggest concern the captives and broken hearts, or is it our reputations and keeping the boat afloat?

What was the difference between Joshua and Caleb and the rest of their generation? Numbers 14:24 (NIV) says this, *"My servant Caleb has a different spirit and follows me wholeheartedly"*. Numbers 32:12 (NIV) says none of their generation would see the Promised Land, *"except Caleb and Joshua, for they followed the Lord wholeheartedly"*. This testimony suggests they were more than merely radical young men. When Caleb was eighty-five years old, He said to Joshua,

> *I am still as strong today as I was in the day Moses sent me, as my strength was then, so my strength is now for war and for going out and coming in. Now then, give me this country about which the Lord spoke on that day, for you heard on that day that Anakim were there, with great fortified cities; perhaps the Lord will be with me, and I shall drive them out as the Lord has spoken* (Numbers 14:11-12, NAS).

At his advanced age, Caleb was still a risk taker. He was willing to leave the prior successes behind and lead the tribe of Judah into a new country, with new enemies. Why? Because he was still basing his life on what the Lord directed him to do. He was still being led by vision from the Lord, rather than general principles or merely good theology!

Fathers Preparing Children

At the beginning of this chapter, I said Church leaders today must go beyond being caught up in the current prophetic fervor; strategically, we need to synchronize our preparations with God's. What the younger generation needs is visible, living examples of mature, Godly men in leadership who, rather than maintaining the status quo, base their lives on the Spirit's leading.

But part of that need transcends role models; as intimate relationships are developed, three things occur: impartation of character, love, and healing. Overall, the Church leaders to emerge as time goes on are, more than anything else, going to be real "father figures" who closely take interest in what God is doing with the next generation.

This is precisely what God is currently doing. Jesus was the perfect example, for in addition to fulfilling His own ministry, the cross, He also prepared His disciples for the day when the Spirit would fall and the Church would explode in growth.

Another example we have of the father figure model is David with his son Solomon. The time came when David prophetically realized the Lord was not going to allow him to be the one to build the temple (Interestingly, David found this out through prophetic ministry, namely Nathan the prophet, rather than through his own wisdom).

David was at the peak of his powers and popularity. It was his intention to build this magnificent temple as a place of worship for the Lord. But the most significant part of David's life was his intimacy with the Lord, so even though he was king, he backed off from his own plans and listened to what the Lord said. The Lord informed Him that since David's hands were bloody from being a man of war he was not the one to build the temple (I Chronicles 22:6-18). Whoever was going to build the temple would have to be a man of peace (I Chronicles 28:3).

This is exactly what God is bringing about in the Church today. Too much sin, warfare, and bloodshed exist within the Church because of leadership's rampant spiritual pride and heavy, self-righteous, judgmental attitudes. The Lord is raising up a generation of leaders, who, as a result of intimacy with God, are going to be walking in obedience and humility. These will be the peacemakers.

David was told by the Lord that one of his sons would build the temple. God said, *"I have chosen him to be my son, and I will be his Father"* (I Chronicles 28:6, NIV). This, again, is a picture of what God is doing today, building up a generation of those who have a childlike relationship with God the Father. This is going to be the generation that, symbolically speaking, is going to build God's temple. As Habakkuk says, *"The earth will be filled with the knowledge of the glory of the Lord, as the waters cover the sea"* (Habakkuk 2:14, NIV).

So rather than sit back, content to continue on in the momentum of what God was already doing in his life, David began to prepare Solomon for the building of the temple. David gathered 1,000,000 talents of silver and 100,00 talents of gold. Then he gathered iron, bronze, stone, carpenters, stone cutters, and ironworkers. He spared no expense, because he considered it more important to bless what God was blessing than to do his own thing.

Three qualities are required for the type of leaders we need for the Church today . First, we need leaders who are absolutely committed to seeking first the kingdom of God, rather than the kingdom of the Church, or the kingdom of man. Second, we need leaders who are risk takers - men and women who are not concerned about either their reputations or their own successes. These will be leaders like Jesus:

> *Your attitude should be the same as that of Christ Jesus, who, being in very nature God, did not consider equality with God something to be grasped, but made himself nothing, taking the very nature of a servant, being made in human likeness.*
> *And being found in appearance as a man, he humbled himself and became obedient to death - even death on a cross!* (Phil. 2:5-8, NIV)

Third, we need leaders who not only seek what God is saying, but, like David with Solomon, begin to prepare the future generation of leaders for what God has in store. Let us begin to focus on what God is doing in the long run. And just as God is doing now, let us begin to pour ourselves into the younger generation to prepare them for building the temple. Let us equip a generation of peacemakers who will be known as the children of God. Let us forget about the status quo and let us, as Jesus says, *"Permit the children to come to Me, and do not hinder them; for the kingdom of God belongs to such as these"* (Luke 18:16, NAS).

"For the vision is yet for an appointed time; it hastens toward the goal, and it will not fail. Though it tarries, wait for it, for it will certainly come; it will not delay" (Habakkuk 2:3, NAS).

Chapter Four

Eating the Food Jesus Ate

The hour has come for the Son of Man to be glorified. I tell you the truth, unless a kernel of wheat falls to the ground and dies, it remains only a single seed. But if it dies, it produces many seeds. The man who loves his life will lose it, while the man who hates his life in this world will keep it for eternal life. (John 12:23-25, NIV)

Jesus spoke these words knowing He would soon be arrested, beaten, mocked, and then crucified for a people who had and would again reject Him. When He was in the Garden wrestling with His humanity, His singular focus on pleasing the Father made the difference in His decision-making process. What motivated His life and actions were His love for the Father and His desire to obey Him.

We are in a time today when the Father is preparing the Church for battle. The Captain of the Lord's Hosts is speaking to the hearts of the children, calling us into the Father's battle formation, as when the Lord gave Joshua a strategy of worship to bring down Jericho (Joshua 5:13-15).

The order and formation the Lord is establishing for the end-time Church is going to be prophetic. By that, I mean the Church will change from operating on human wisdom to operating on the wisdom gained from listening to and then obeying what the Lord has to say. It will not be an easy transition, for God's order is often contrary to our understanding and wisdom. This is because God's ways are above our ways and His thoughts are above our thoughts (Isaiah 55:8). Too seldom, then, do we recognize the beginning of wisdom is to fear God.

For many Church leaders, the 90's will be a time of incredible upheaval, because as Jesus cleansed the temple, so God is cleansing us in order to make us into a house of prayer. The sacrifices of our works we bring into the temple are no longer going to be valued. This should come as no surprise, since many of us are familiar with Samuel's words to King Saul: *"To obey is better than sacrifice"* (I Samuel 15:22, NIV).

But do we really understand the effect the forthcoming upheaval will have on our relationship with God the Father? The Bible promises specific rewards for those who remain faithful. Matthew 25, in the parable of the stewards and the talents, makes an interesting point concerning the master's rewards for obedience. For the two stewards who had employed the talents given them, not only were they given more responsibility but they were told to enter into the joy of their master. The shared joy was given as a reward for obedience rather than purely as a result of what the servants had accomplished.

Where is Our Food Coming From?

In John, chapter four, the disciples return to Jesus with food, but He tells them He has food they do not know of. When they become confused, Jesus responds to them by saying, *"My food is to do the will of Him who sent Me"* (John 4:34, NIV). He was telling the disciples what it was He actually lived on and which nourished Him.

The question for us is what are we being nourished on? It is common to hear cliché proclamations such as "I am living to glorify my Lord Jesus Christ," or "I have received a manifesto from God to preach the gospel to the nations." To a certain degree, these types of statements sound very spiritual, especially when large sacrifices are made. But the question stands: why are we doing what we are?

The question is important because the Lord is sifting the hearts as never before. If God's hand is visibly going to increase in our lives, our hearts will have to be pure. Purity is essential because only the pure in heart will see God. It is possible to end up having our reward on earth, but then be bankrupt at the judging of the saints.

Too often, the pure in heart receive criticism from within the church. For instance, when the woman washed Jesus' feet with costly perfume, the disciples were critical, because the perfume could have provided a lot of money for the poor. On the other hand, the needs of ministry, just like the needs of the poor, are always with us, and God definitely wants us to be ministering His love and compassion to the world in practical ways. But as far as God is concerned, there is a greater priority than good works: the greatest commandment is to love God first.

Our love affair with God has to be the impetus behind our lives, and then out of that love comes His perfect will revealed. This is what provides our direction and satisfaction.

Recently, while flipping through the television channels, I caught a few minutes of a show featuring a well-known Christian pastor and teacher. He was making final preparations for a spiritual warfare conference centered around prayer for a certain city. In a very theatrical style, he dramatically stated God had created his wife and him for this particular last days' ministry.

Of course, God has ordained good works that we should walk in them, but that is not **why** He created us. God created us that we might know Him, love Him, and be loved by Him. There is a God-created hunger for Him within us which cannot be satisfied by anything but God Himself. Jesus is not **about** "the Life" He **is** "the Life," and not even good works - as necessary and fulfilling as they are - can be a substitute for God.

Not by Bread Alone

Undeniably, for us in the Western world, our understanding of the Bible and God is permeated by our culture's materialistic value system.   We feed on numbers, outward success, and the accolades of man. Jesus, however, is quite unequivocal when He states:

> *Not everyone who says to me, 'Lord, Lord will enter the kingdom of heaven, but only he who does the will of my Father who is in heaven. Many will say to me on that day, 'Lord, Lord, did we not prophesy in your name, and in your name drive out demons and perform many miracles?' Then I will tell them plainly, "I never knew you. Away from me, you evildoers!* (Matthew 7:21-23, NIV)

"Evildoers" here does not refer to overt sinners, but to those who practice Christ-like ministry without intimacy with God. That healings and deliverances take place is almost irrelevant. Jesus precedes this passage by qualifying what a true prophetic ministry is, and, interestingly, He never says anything about whether or not the prophet is highly accurate or not. The point being, the obvious and the given cannot be used to determine success in the Kingdom, because God sees way beyond the outward appearances.

The question is this: what is God really after in our service to Him? I am not trying to condone failure, laziness, or lame ministry, but I am saying that measuring success only by the yardstick of size and numbers can be very dangerous if not demonic. Sooner or later, we need to come to the realization David did: the true sacrifice God wants from us goes way beyond money, time, or materialism. God desires truth in our innermost being, and that truth is Jesus.

If, through our cultural mind-set, we attempt to understand the gospel, then the goal of Christianity is reduced to nothing more than making it to heaven and/or a position in ministry. Heaven becomes a home or mansion, and ministry is a position or title. In this realm, we work for money, which in turn allows us to purchase and then possess things; for in our culture, success is measured by personal power and the quality and quantity of our possessions.

The problem is if we do not experience the Father's heart, our personal identities and security continue to be controlled by what we can achieve, build, and obtain. With this mind-set, little is changed in our value process. We, perhaps, have changed ethics and morals, but we still operate out of a value system in which bigger is better, and everything counts in large amounts.

Jesus, a master at parabolic teaching, said, *"Where your treasure is, there your heart will be also"* (Matthew 6:21, NIV). This statement is not only true figuratively, but, for the Christian, it is also true literally. In spite of this truth, the world's continued influence can affect us, and our motivations can still be based on what we can accomplish, rather than focused on what God values foremost: our hearts.

We might actually be attempting to serve God but be completely ignorant of what the Lord would like to say to us. Spiritual deafness can result if our hearts are focused on anything in Christianity other than God Himself. Frequently, we ask one another, "What is the Lord saying to you?" We speak about the good things happening but seldom tell what the Lord is actually **saying**. Frighteningly, we sometimes do not even realize we have not addressed the question.

In the final analysis, our motivation process has to change if we are going to continue on in the outpouring of the Holy Spirit.

Because God gives grace to the humble, our motivations will change when we submit truly to God's sovereignty. This submission is vital, because many areas of the world are already coming into times of God's sovereign movement.

Sovereign times mean times when the Lord requires very little work from us, unlike times past when much work was required for a little harvest. It is like the second time when the Hebrew people had no water in the wilderness in Numbers 20. The first time, Moses worked a little - the Lord told him to hit a rock with his staff. But by the second occurrence, Israel had a deeper revelation of God and there was less room for man's efforts. Therefore, God told Moses just to speak to the rock. Ignoring God - for Moses preferred to operate from tradition - he hit the rock with his staff. God judged Moses, and he was not allowed to enter into the Promised Land.

God's call is to believe Him and to live by every word proceeding from His mouth.

Coming to the Table with Jesus

In the book of Revelation, chapter 3, the church of Laodicea symbolizes the Church today, the end-time Church. We lean towards lukewarm rather than hot, and prideful and arrogant rather than humble and compassionate. The Lord, however, as a loving Father, desires to heat us up. The fuel for the fire is intimacy with Him. Jesus finishes His rebuke of the Laodicean church with an invitation: *"Behold, I stand at the door and knock; if anyone hears My voice and opens the door, I will come in to him, and will dine with him, and he with Me"* - the operative word is "hears" *(Revelation 3:20, NAS).*

For Christian leaders today, recognizing we are in a prophetic time is not enough. Hearing prophesies is not enough either. The time is not just for prophets, the time is for a prophetic church. This is the latter fulfillment of the time Joel speaks of: *"Your sons and daughters will prophesy, your old men will dream dreams, your young men will see visions. Even on my servants, both men and women, I will pour out my Spirit"* (Joel 2:28-29).

Scripture gives a pattern of times leaders were invited to sit and eat in God's presence. At these meals, revelation was the main food on the menu. Exodus 24: 9-11 (NAS), says:

> *Moses went up with Aaron, Nadab and Abihu, and seventy of the elders of Israel, and they saw the God of Israel; and under His feet there appeared to be a pavement of sapphire, as clear as the sky itself, Yet He did not stretch out His hand against the nobles of the sons of Israel; and they beheld God, and they ate and drank.*

Saul's history as king of Israel began with sitting down with Samuel the prophet and eating a reserved choice portion. Jesus told His disciples He had been longing to sit with them for the last supper. What was it that was really being served at these meals?

The outpouring of the Holy Spirit now coming is not just a release of power or anointing; it is God's manifest presence with us, the Immanuel. And as His presence increases in our lives and assemblies, the first real fruit is going to be humility, especially among leadership. My friend Hans Lundahl, a teacher in Sweden, defines

49

humility as being flexible. We must be flexible to the point we are willing to bend and even abandon our own agendas and do God's will instead of our own presuppositions and traditions.

Walking with God

Both Moses and Joshua experienced just such an important turning point in flexible humility in their lives. Their pivotal moments came when they had direct encounters with the Lord. They came to an understanding God is an incredible God who wants to do things His way. The one thing both Moses and Joshua experienced during these pivotal encounters with the Lord was this: they were told to take off their shoes because they were on holy ground - in the presence of the Lord (Exodus 3 and John 5 respectively).

One reason God told them to take off their shoes was because He desired them to relax and freely spend time in His presence. Like the invitation to the Church of Laodicea, God wanted Moses and later Joshua to sit down with Him and spend intimate time together.

The Lord desires us to learn to commune with Him and to enjoy His presence. David says, in Psalm 16:11, (NAS): *"Thou will make known to me the path of life; In Thy presence is fullness of joy; In Thy right hand there are pleasures forever."* This is what Jesus meant when He said we should be a called a "House of Prayer".

In scripture, feet often symbolize taking forth the gospel. Paul exhorted the Ephesian Church to put shoes on the feet of the gospel of peace. In an earlier instance, Isaiah 52:7 (NAS) reads, *"How lovely on the mountains are the feet of him who brings good news, who announces peace and brings good news of happiness, Who announces salvation, and says to Zion, 'Your God reigns'."*

50

I believe the pavement of sapphire Israel's elders saw under the Lord's feet in Exodus 24 is the "Highway of Holiness" described in Isaiah 35. Isaiah said fools would not walk on this highway. Now, Jesus told the disciples they were already clean because of the Word spoken to them in John 13. But, evidently, one area of cleansing still remained, and that was their feet. So at the Last Supper, Jesus stripped down to a towel and began to wash their feet. When Peter asked Jesus to also wash his hands and head Jesus replied, *"He who has bathed needs only to wash his feet."*.

Like the disciples, we, too, are clean because we have heard the Word and have come into the Lamb's blood-cleansing. But our feet are dirty from walking by our own directions and doing our own things, even if we have done so in the name of Jesus. The time is now here for us to walk hand in hand and heart to heart with the Lord.

> *I will take hold of your hand. I will keep you and will make you to be a covenant for the people and a light for the Gentiles, to open eyes that are blind, to free captives from prison and to release from the dungeon those who sit in darkness.* (Isaiah 42:6-7, NIV).

To Whom Much is Given, Much is Required

The Lord is raising a new spiritual generation of leaders today. These leaders for the new wine will be flexible and humble instead of stiff and proud. Without a doubt, prophetic times call for radical obedience.

This radical obedience is clearly illustrated in 1 Kings, chapter 13. The Lord sent a young prophet from Judah to Bethel [Significantly, the root word for "Judah" means "deep celebration with praise and reverence to the Lord," and the word "Bethel" means "house of the Lord." These words are important for us today because restoration is going to originate out of our love affair with God]. But the young prophet, after obeying the Lord and bringing restoration to Israel, was then disobedient and took advice of an older prophet and ate the food of man.

The older prophet had probably never seen the Lord moving so sovereignly and did not consider complete obedience a matter of importance. That disobedience cost the young prophet his life, because since he represented the sovereign King that sovereignty had to begin in his life.

Today, before the return of our Lord Jesus, the Father is quite committed to reaching the multitudes with His love. Decreasingly, will "churchianity" and spiritually void Church practices be the norm. The King is on the move, and those moving with Him are going to have to be walking in revelation of the "I AM". Judgment is already on the Church, and it is going to increase throughout the next years. This is because prophetic revelation, especially about God, does not come without a stiff price tag.

In the late `80s and early '90's, the Lord dealt with hidden sins of the flesh and money, but now God is dealing strongly with hypocrisy and false motives. We must realize there will be consequences for these sins. Indeed, Jesus spoke about eyes to see and ears to hear when He said, *"To whoever has, to him shall more be given, and he shall have an abundance: but whoever does not have, even what he has shall be taken away from him"* (Matthew 13:12, NAS).

Anointing is greatly going to increase the next several years, but, for many, even what anointing and revelation they have now will be lost, if they fail to respond to the Father's heart. Those who do not repent and return to their first love will lose their lamp stand.

When Jesus criticized, it was not prostitutes, thieves, and outcasts He condemned - it was hypocrisy in the leadership. Soon, there will be nowhere to hide in the Kingdom of God. The day will come when the long list of people who are in ministry now will drastically change, and some God will take out of leadership. The Lord, in His mercy, will take some home, rather than continue to allow them to mislead His people, misrepresent His throne, and especially deny His heart.

Moses never entered into the sins of his fellow Hebrews. But his disobedience of what God had spoken to him cost him his life (Numbers 20:12), just as with the young prophet. The Lord considered Moses' disobedience to His directions blatant sin. According to Numbers 12, Moses was the only man God spoke openly to, even mouth to mouth. God took that intimacy with Moses very seriously. To whom much is given much is required.

Finally, it is imperative we start listening to the Father, blessing what **He** is blessing, instead of continually asking Him to bless **our** plans and endless programs. But such listening begins and ends in our hearts. It is our love the Father is after. That is where our values and decision-making processes need to change. Then obedience out of revelation will follow. *"I tell you the truth, the Son can do nothing by himself; he can do only what he sees his Father doing, because whatever the Father does the Son also does"* (John 5:19, NIV).

And, again, *"Serve Him with wholehearted devotion and with a willing mind, for the Lord searches every heart and understands every motive behind the thoughts. If you seek him, he will be found by you,"* (1 Chronicles 28:9, NIV).

Chapter Five

Love Versus Pharisaism

"Destroy this temple, and in three days I will raise it again", Jesus replied to his critics (John 2:19, NIV). More than responding to the questions in the Temple, He was issuing a challenge to Satan, not for the first time. Similarly, God said to Satan, *"Have you considered My servant Job? There is no one like him on the earth, a blameless and upright man, fearing God and turning away from evil"* (Job 1:8, NAS).

With both Jesus and Job, the Father, in His sovereignty, used Satan to accomplish His perfect will. In His infinite wisdom and love, God takes the best He has and allows Satan to do his worst. Then, out of the ash heaps, God glorifies His name.

This is the pattern of what is coming on the Church. As with Jesus, God is allowing the powerful spirit of Pharisaism to do its worst. The result is going to be a people who are broken and humble before God's throne. A people who will tremble at His word. The tables are being turned on Christians who have made idols out of theology, order, and tradition. Out of the confusion and desperation, a cry is coming for the reality of God's Spirit and love in the Church.

The ones to stand are going to be those who realize they are in a pit. The Lord will place their feet on the rock of revelation. The ones who endure will be the flexible, the humble, the ones who learn to pray, "Not my will, but Father, your will be done."

Blessed are the flexible, for they shall bend and not be broken. The stiff and proud are going to be spit out of the Lord's mouth.

We are quickly entering tremendous warfare which is going to devastate some churches so thoroughly even the dust will be scattered. Others will be broken to pieces. But those pieces will be living stones, smooth and conformed to the person of Jesus. They will be stones which fit together and complement one another in unity, for building an end-time house of prayer. These workable stones will be those who humble themselves before the Lord and learn to tremble at His voice.

This may not sound like much of a method for church growth, but it is God's method of kingdom growth. In order to work the coming harvest, we are about to experience an unbelievable filling of God's Spirit. In the Church's present condition, the gates are not only somewhat shut to the presence of God but also to the unchurched, who are hungry for the reality of God. Not only are most leaders not entering into the Kingdom, but they stand at the gate and keep out those who would come in (Matthew 23:13).

The choice before us right now is this: we can either continue to try to operate out of a Pharisaical understanding of God and what He is doing, or we can drink the cup the Father hands us. The only way we can glorify the Father is to die to our own wills.

Whose Church is it Anyway?

The question is who is going to be on the throne of the Church? Is it going to be our intellectual, religious attempts at control, or is it going to be the voice of the Spirit as we seek first the King? As every Christian leader should know, the Spirit cannot be controlled. If He could be controlled, He would not be the Spirit of the Lord God Jehovah. The Pharisaical Church, by nature, would rather fight to death than lose control and order. As Proverbs 14:4 implies, God would rather have a mess - which indicates a whole lot of life happening -

and then clean up...than have everything nice, polite, and religiously controlled.

God is committed to our growing into peacemaking sons. In His sovereignty, He will use an enemy of the kingdom, Pharisaism, to shake us, break us, and empty us out so He can fill us up. Just as Jesus said, in Matthew 10:36, our enemies will be of our own household. No one really knows our weakness like a family member, so it is going to be those who think they know us best, and who really believe they are doing best, whom the Lord is going to use to take us through the refiner's fire and bring us under His control.

A Prophetic Invitation to Death

In setting us free of religious strongholds, God is calling us to radical obedience. This obedience leads to death and then, in turn, brings forth eternal life. Jesus knew this exact process when he said:

> *The hour has come for the Son of Man to be glorified. I tell you the truth, unless a kernel of wheat falls to the ground and dies, it remains only a single seed. But if it dies, it produces many seeds. The man who loves his life will lose it, while the man who hates his life in this world will keep it for eternal life. Whoever serves me must follow me* (John 12:23-26, NIV).

Jesus, out of radical love and full knowledge of what to expect, subjected Himself to the complete will of the Father. As Isaiah prophesied, Jesus was like a sheep silent before His shearers (Isaiah 53:7).

Jesus, in Matthew 16, prophetically told Peter He would build His Church on "a rock of revelation" - hearing from the Father. But Jesus also told Peter he was going to be sifted as wheat (Luke 22:31). At that point, Peter was bound and blinded by spiritual pride. Not only was he puffed up by his faith and commitment, but he was so confident in his wisdom that he, under demonic leading, actually rebuked Jesus.

With Peter, unlike Jesus, Satan had a legal right to sift him because of his spiritual pride. The Peter who emerged on the beach with Jesus, after the resurrection, was a Peter broken and humble - a man whom God could trust on the day of Pentecost (John 21).

Like Peter, many leaders today have a prophetic expectation of God's using them. But before that can be a reality, those leaders are going to have to die to self, for God is opposed to the proud. The death process will be so complete we will no longer have any confidence in our abilities and gifts to build the kingdom.

As Jesus went through the fire of dying to himself, so are we. Jesus said, *"My heart is troubled, and what shall I say? 'Father, save me from this hour'? No, it was for this very reason I came to this hour. Father, glorify your name!" (John 12:27-28, NIV)*. We too will end up at a place of hopelessness with only enough faith to say, "Father into your hands I commit my being".

When we come to the point where we only want the Father's love, wisdom, and sovereignty, we will be where revelation transcends ideals and moves beyond agendas and into extending life to for hurt and broken. Such transcendent revelation is essential because authority comes not from teaching or anointing, but from revelation, which releases authority, which releases power.

The Issue is Love

Not only is it necessary for us to go through the refiner's fire, but because of sin in the Church, Satan has the legal right to demand permission from the Father to test us. God, in His sovereign timing and wisdom, is at this moment, I believe, giving permission to Satan to begin. Jesus said in a time of wars and rumors of wars, earthquakes, famines and droughts, most people's love would grow cold and many would fall away, hate one another, and deliver up one another in betrayal (Matthew 24).

These calamities, although already in evidence, are about to be greatly multiplied. Christians and leaders who are primarily criticizing, attacking, and condemning other Christians are going to increase in their vehemence. Leaders will attack leaders - even within specific fellowships - to the point many Churches are going to fall apart purely from the warfare within. This is already taking place, but it is going to accelerate.

Sins which the Bible clearly labels as punishable by hell, such as slander, gossip, and lying are going to increase in the Church for two basic reasons: first, the Lord wants to move sovereignly; that is, not by our efforts or plans, but by His power and strategy. Pharisaical leaders will be more and more provoked by what they cannot control, understand, or duplicate. As Isaiah says in chapter 3, when God overtly moves, what He does is a *"stone of stumbling, a rock of offense"* to the natural, religious mind. 1 Corinthians 2:10-14 (NIV) says this:

> *The Spirit searches all things even the deep things of God...No one knows the thoughts of God except the Spirit of God. We have not received the spirit of the world but the Spirit who is from God, that we may understand what God has freely given us. This is what we speak, not in words taught us by human wisdom but in words taught by the Spirit, expressing spiritual truths in spiritual words. The man without the Spirit*

does not accept the things that come from the Spirit of God, for they are foolishness to him, and he cannot understand them, because they are spiritually discerned.

Second, Pharisaical warfare is more than an attitude. It is a demonic force that can powerfully deceive when we mainly trust in our own understanding. People will be more and more given over to criticism and pride, preferring the **form** of godliness to the reality of God. The deception will be so strong some will be in direct disobedience to the Bible but still attempt to biblically justify their malevolent attacks on other Christians.

The hard-core evidence of the Pharisaical spirit is when Christians, especially leaders, are no longer focused on extending life and resolving issues. Instead, they judge, condemn, and destroy one another. If Jesus' standards for New Testament prophets were applied to some teaching ministries today, they would be seen for what they are - the fruit speaks for itself. When orthodoxy, traditions, and peripheral doctrines are more important than love and acceptance of brothers, Pharisaism is in control. The problem is, as Jesus said in Matthew 24, love has grown cold.

Spiritual discernment comes from the heart, not the head. Nevertheless, a great number of church leaders operate more from natural wisdom than by spiritual discernment. This is because in our priorities we have valued theology and doctrine more than prayer and worship. To many churches, prayer and worship are merely programs to go through as understood concepts.

This practice has brought present church leadership to the place of the leadership of Jesus' time: knowing the scriptures but not recognizing the Messiah - ignorance to the point where the Spirit's actions are called demonic.

It may be helpful to note the difference between a "Jezebel spirit" and a Pharisaical spirit. The Pharisaical is, in its own mind, completely committed to doing the things of God. The problem is the Pharisaical mind confuses the things of God for God Himself. Relationship, compassion, and grace are exchanged for performance, control and order.

The Jezebel spirit, on the other hand, is as witchcraft in the body of Christ. Using spiritual gifts, manipulation, and power, the person under a Jezebel influence is fixed on gaining personal power, glory or money. Both, however, are against the prophetic moving of the Holy Spirit, because the Spirit brings liberty and discernment to God's people to come out of control and/or fear.

Religious Bondage or Spiritual Freedom

The current prophetic activity is exemplified in 2 Samuel 6. After David had come into kingship, his heart's desire was to retrieve the Ark, which symbolized the presence of God.

Many of the future Joshuas and Calebs are now coming into strong leadership anointing. And, like David, they are desiring to bring back to the Church the real presence of God, as the early Church experienced Him.

As David brought the Ark to the city, the Israelites worshipped the Lord the best they knew how. Irreverently touching the symbolic presence of God, a man called Uzzah (meaning strength of man) died on the threshing floor.

Uzzah's death is what the '90's are all about: crossing the threshing floor in reverence and coming into a place of true worship in Spirit and revelatory truth. The Lord is teaching us to *"work out [our] salvation with fear and trembling, for it is God who works in you to will and to act according to his good purpose* (as opposed to ours)" (Phil. 2:12-13, NIV). David, in frustration and anger over loosing his man Uzzah, left the Ark, but was soon back, provoked to jealousy because the farmer who owned the threshing floor was being blessed by the presence of the Lord.

For those of you who feel like your whole life is one big threshing floor, have hope. God is definitely preparing you for a day of Pentecost in which His glory will move. The key to coming out of the threshing floor successfully is in what David then began to do.

This time, when David came again with the Ark, the people were not just worshipping as tradition dictated. They got radical in demonstrating love and thanks to the Lord. They went six paces, made a sacrifice to the Lord, and then David danced in the streets with all of His might.

It is not a question of dancing or not but a question of losing ourselves in Him. God is calling us to break past the limited understanding of Him we are capable of intellectually, and to begin to treat Him as God. The Pharisaical power over the Church is broken when we say, "Father, your will, not mine!"

In the midst of David's dancing, a Pharisaical spirit arose in Michal, David's wife. She felt embarrassed by David's childlike behavior in the streets. She just could not relate to David's being consumed with joy over the presence of the Lord.

Her reaction is a lot like that of Christians today, who have little tolerance for prayer and worship. One of the real differences between people who are seeking first the kingdom of God and people who are focused on churchianity is this: kingdom people love to worship and pray to the Father, while religious people prefer endless activity.

People who have experienced revelation of the Father, as Ephesians 1:17-18 talks about, become like the woman who used her hair to spread costly perfume on Jesus' feet. Conversely, many others consider it a waste when that time, energy, and money could be spent on more programs. In the spiritual realm, on the other hand, anything not coming out of prayer and worship seems a waste!

Michal, our example of Pharisaism, then rebuked David. From that time on she was under a curse - she remained childless, unfruitful. Churches and Christians today refusing the call of the Spirit to renew their love affair with God will lose their lamp stands - their witness to the world and their ability to exercise spiritual discernment. Many are at a place already where, in the name of defending theological values, they are becoming anti-biblical in their intent and actions. *"Whoever has will be given more...whoever does not have, even what he has will be taken from him"* (Matthew 13:22, NIV) as their hearts get hardened.

Lessons From the Threshing Floor

In the face of the present warfare, we have only one recourse: to get on our faces before the Father. The level of spiritual warfare, especially divisive criticism and rejection within the Church, is going to increase dramatically. If we are not on our knees, in love, before the Father, we will find ourselves either on our backs, in fear, before the enemy, or in growing pride and arrogance!

Isaiah 30:15 says, *"In repentance and rest you will be saved, in quietness and trust is your strength."* Through the power of repentance, on our knees, we can be free to stand before our enemies. Though the power of the Lord's calm, we can be free to storm the gates of Hell.

Warfare Strategy Against Pharisaism

When telling the disciples He was leaving them for a place they could not immediately follow, Jesus said, *"A new commandment I give to you: Love one another. As I have loved you, so you must love one another. By this all men will know that you are My disciples, if you love one another"*.

If we are going to come into the Spirit's movement, we must delve deeper into love and not allow our hearts to be hardened. This is the only way to overcome Pharisaical warfare.

Just as God allowed Jesus to be struck down by Pharisaical warfare, He will allow many leaders to be struck down and the sheep to be scattered. For some, the warfare of loveless criticism, rejection, and condemnation is going to come from ones we have shared our cup with. This is why it is going to be so intense! At the core of the intensity is the issue of love; if we lose our love for God's people, we have lost the battle. If we have lost our love for our brother, we are no longer loving God.

Four principles will arm us against the Pharisaical warfare coming at us through people in our own churches or circles.

First, we need to remember who the enemy is and is not. We do not fight against flesh and blood, but against demonic principalities. So love has to rule. That means we pray for our brother who attacks us, and, as much as possible, be peacemakers - Sons of God. Remember, usually people who hurt others do so because they themselves are hurting.

Second, we are to walk in humility rather than in self-righteousness. Often, even when an accusation or slander against us is wrong, there may be a grain of truth to it. If we are before the Father in humility, we can be quick to discern the truth, repent where necessary, and minister love. In the event the criticism is true, rather than trying to justify ourselves, we need do what Jesus said: "Settle matters quickly with your adversary," so we are not judged (Matthew 5:25, NIV). Like my friend Ron Allen says, "The most humble guy wins". Being humble does not mean denying what is true or backing off of the Father's will; rather, it means maintaining love at the cost of personal pride.

Third, we need to let God be our defense. Our strength is in quietness and trust (Isaiah 30:15), not in ourselves. When our minds are focused on the Father, His perfect peace can override any situation (Isaiah 26:3). And then, in humility, we can hear from the Spirit how to pray, and receive the Father's wisdom about what steps to take. For further reading, see Numbers 12:1-15.

Fourth, 1 Kings 8:35 tells us when we come before the Lord we are to be aware of the afflictions of our heart. When we approach God in humility, there is a freedom in our lives to allow past bitterness, unforgiveness, or sin to come into the light.

To overcome the coming warfare, we need to appropriate Jesus' payment for sins, so Satan can have nothing on us. *"In repentance and rest is your salvation"* (Isaiah 30:15). " And again, this is what the Lord says: *"Heaven is my throne, and the earth is my footstool. Where is the house you will build for me? Where will my resting place be? Has not my hand made all these things, and so they came into being?"* Finally, the Lord declares, *"This is the one I esteem: he who is humble and contrite in spirit, and trembles at my word"* (Isaiah 66:1-2, NIV).

Chapter Six

A Jericho Year

Psalm 68:7-10 (NAS) reads:

> *O God, when Thou did go forth before thy people, When Thou did march through the wilderness, the earth quaked; the heavens also dropped rain at the presence of God; Sinai itself quaked at the presence of God, the God of Israel. Thou did shed abroad a plentiful rain, O God; Thou did confirm their inheritance, when it was parched. Thy creatures settled in it; Thou did provide in Thy goodness for the poor, O God.*

Despite culturally relevant programs and methodology of the contemporary Church, only a sovereign move of God's presence will shake the demonic realm and release the rains of revival on world cultures.

When Adam and Eve decided to "be like God," they exchanged a relationship of childlike dependence on the Father for an adult/adult relationship where they could be in control of their lives. Part of the curse they stepped into when exiting the garden was to face responsibility for their own needs. By the sweat of their brow they had to work in order to survive.

In like manner, it is only by the sweat of Jesus' blood, in His childlike obedience to the Father in the second garden, that man can leave the slavery of performance and come again into a childlike dependence on the Father's power and provision. As

Paul said (Romans 8:15, NIV) *"You did not receive a spirit that makes you a slave again to fear, but you received the spirit of sonship and by Him we cry "Abba Father!."*

As a consequence of the fall, man has had a major conflict between trustingly obeying God and doing things out of man's own wisdom and strength. As Isaiah said, *"In repentance and rest is your salvation, in quietness and trust is your strength, but you would have none of it"* (Isaiah 30:15, NIV).

Frequently there is great conflict of letting God be God in the Church, where religious spirits and people sometimes prefer religious activity to spiritual worship.

Primarily, religious activity gets in the way of the Holy Spirit's movement; this is the "Martha syndrome". Man, oftentimes with good intentions, falls into the trap of doing busywork for God rather than listening and acting out of obedience. We must not forget, however, to obey is always better than just giving God our religious sacrifices (I Samuel 15:22). He does not need them anyway.

Laying our busyness aside, we must respond to the Holy Spirit. In the last few years, as many leaders are aware, the Holy Spirit has been releasing within the Body of Christ two heart cries for prayer and worship. Both are completely central to the last days' Church. By these main disciplines, we experience communication with the Father and know His presence and specific will. They are the keys to intimacy with God which will allow the contemporary Church to enter into what the Father is doing.

If one single verse captures the Spirit's message to the present Church, it is Psalm 46:10 (NIV): *"Be still, and know that I am God; I will be exalted among the Nations, I will be exalted in the earth."* Most of the time, when God is overtly on the move, He deliberately operates in seemingly childish and offensive ways. This is because the kingdom is being built on a rock of revelation which is a "stone of stumbling and a rock of offense" (I Peter 2:8, NAS) to a religious paradigm.

At the end of 1992 I prayed about the year to come. I heard the Lord say it was to be a Jericho year - meaning a year of breakthrough in radical worship - for many churches. The word "radical" in Latin is the word "roots," meaning core beginnings. In essence, the Lord was calling the Church back to its roots: a radical first love of Jesus. The call was to desire foremost to worship and obey Him, instead of focusing on religiously fulfilling the status quo.

This was the preparation Israel underwent prior to marching on Jericho. The Israelites' worship really began when they sent out spies years before (Numbers 23). Among the twelve tribes, only Joshua and Caleb had faith God could give them victory over the giants in the land.

As previously stated, many Joshuas and Calebs are being released now to lead a more obedient generation of people. The Church renewal of the 60's and 70's was powerful, but many of the people of the renewal movement still lived their lives without really seeking first the King's will for their lives. It is going to be the children of the renewal generation that will, metaphorically speaking, take the Church across the Jordan.

The radical call on the next generation is a stumbling block for the older generation as it looks at all the current cultural rebellion. But, the inverse of what Jesus said in Luke 7:47 is, "Those who are forgiven much, love much".

A Time of Circumcision

Upon crossing the Jordan, the Israelites immediately purified themselves by circumcising the men. Even though they were of a generation raised in freedom, the outward sign of Egypt - slavery - was still on them and from this they needed to be cleansed.

For the last few years, many Christians have been going through a similar process of spiritual circumcision. Our circumcision is not of the flesh, as was the Israelites', but of the heart. Though all Christians are "saved" by the blood of the Lamb and are going to heaven, much of the Church today is still bound by attitudes and values of the world, which makes it difficult for us to serve God freely. As Jesus said, *"No one can serve two masters"* (Matthew 6:24, NIV).

In this period of restoration, the Lord, by grace, has initially ordained a time for us to respond to His heart. This is a period of grace on top of grace, as it were, in which we can choose to fall on the rock and be broken, as opposed to later on when the rock will fall on us if we are not broken and humble us before God and man (Matthew 21:44).

As time elapses (I see about a twelve to fifteen-year period, which is about the same foundational period the first church in Jerusalem experienced), judgment will increase visibly on those of God's household who ignore the voice of the Spirit. As God increasingly allows Satan to sift the Church, anointing and God's provision will lift, and protection against the enemy will lessen. Those not repenting by grace to the voice of the Spirit, God the Father will, in love, discipline.

It is always easier to fall on the rock instead of the rock falling on you. But for those churches responding and returning to their first love, as many did in 1993, they will enjoy breakthroughs in the area of evangelism and seeing some of the enemy's walls come down.

The plan for overthrowing Jericho was not a slick strategy, but, actually, a plan which made no sense to the natural mind. The power was not in the plan but in obediently following what God told Joshua to do. And that began by Joshua receiving a fresh revelation of the Lord, as told in Joshua 5:13-15). Before he could go out against Jericho, it was completely necessary for Joshua to get this deeper revelation of God. His response as he met with the "Captain of the host of the Lord" was to fall down on his face in worship and ask the Lord to speak to Him.

As He did with Joshua, the Lord is now standing between His people and the fortressed walls of the cities around us. And, as in Joshua 5, the Lord is holding a sword in His hand; He is ready for battle. That sword, of course, is the sword of the Spirit which consists of words God speaks to His people.

Like the end-time Church of Laodicea in Revelation 3, the question is "who has the ears to hear what the Spirit is saying to the Church"? The key message to the end-time Church is to get hot before we are spit out of the mouth of the Lord. Because, when it comes to intimacy with God, either we go forward or we fall behind.

For many leaders, even what they have experienced in revelation and discernment will be taken away if they do not respond to God's call to prayer and worship. For 1993, the first six days of the Israelites' silent marching around Jericho with the ark, symbolized the first six months of the year. It was a time of listening to the Lord and allowing Him to give new vision, of going with His presence outside of the four walls of the Church. This was followed by a fresh freedom to take the presence of the Lord public, through praise and worship, in mid-summer. It was a season the Lord sovereignly ordained for His people to come out of the Church's walls and, with the high praise of God on our lips as swords, go forth against the walled fortresses of our cultures.

Proclamation Worship

Since then, in addition to the "March for Jesus" in which many Christians participate annually, God is going to give unique strategies to different Churches about new ways of going forth and proclaiming His glory. Much of it will be public ministry, like aid to the poor and good works, but the heart of it is going to center around worship.

There are many different types of worship, such as intimate worship, singing the Lord's promises, rejoicing in His love, etc. What some call "warfare worship" has been popular in some churches for quite awhile. But proclamation worship, by definition, is a "going forth with a shout" right into the face of the adversaries in the public arena, and proclaiming God's sovereignty and glory over all the earth.

One classic biblical instance demonstrating the relationship between worship, God's presence, and the gospel's growth is in Acts 16, when Paul and Silas were locked up in Philippi. Despite their chains, Paul and Silas engaged in proclamation worship, freely singing praise to God before the other inmates right in the enemy's camp, so to speak. God responded to their worship with a mighty shaking of the prison. Prisoners were set free and many came to accept Jesus. From this we see that when people worship, God shows up, and the kingdom grows.

Of course, worship is not a magic formula for protection. In Paul and Silas' case, their worship invited attack from the enemy. Before their arrest, they had been on their way to "the place of prayer." En route, they were accosted by a slave girl with a spirit of divination. After this girl had hounded them for several days, Paul rebuked the spirit which then left the girl. Consequently, the girl was no longer able to tell fortunes, and her owners lost revenue. In anger, they had Paul and Silas arrested. This parallels our times; the demonic realm is increasingly overt, and the real prince in control over the demonic is the spirit of mammon, or money, at least in our Western culture.

There is an important lesson for us here. Many think if they just pray more everything outwardly will get better. On the contrary, the more we pray the more the demonic realm tries to prevent us from praying. Demonic hindrances will increase, and persecution will increase. God allows this because He wants us to completely depend on Him.

The good news for us, however, is that even as outward situations worsen, we find the Lord's anointing on our lives increases. We come to the place of the disciples in the boat: surrounded by a terrible storm but with Holy Spirit drawing near. The question is which ones are going to stay in the boat in Matthew 14:22, clinging to a false sense of security in the system, and which ones are going to say, "Lord, can we walk with you on the water?" Only one of the disciples dared to get out of the boat.

When we look at the history of the Lord with Israel, we see quite often only the tribe of Judah was spared the judgments on the whole nation. When Israel would pray about which tribe should go first into battle, the Lord would say, "Judah shall go first" (Judges 20:18, and 1:2). It is the Lord's desire that we be like Judah.

The word "Judah" comes from the Hebrew root "yadah." This word has two basic meanings: first, to confess who God is - the absolute king of all that exists, and an all - powerful God of great glory, who is the very definition of love. Second, it means to confess our shortcomings in comparison with our God, for He is a god of complete holiness. Emulating Judah, those who lead the attack against the "walled fortresses" of our cultures are going to be those who learn to worship in the presence of the Spirit of God, in the truth of who He is, and in the reality of who we are in His light.

A hindrance to this type of worship can be spiritual pride. Where spiritual pride is the most upsetting to the Lord is in the area of imagined self-sufficiency. From Satan's and Adam's falls to the posture of many church leaders today, there is a posture of imagined strength, a complete self-confidence in our gifts and abilities. With the utmost presumption, we can feel capable of performing God's work by speaking it into existence without even seeking Him.

Isaiah 66:1-2 makes clear that not those who think they can do it but those who are broken before God are going to be the ones to build the Lord's house. Psalm 127:1 says unless He, the Lord, is the builder, we labor in vain.

Like Paul and Silas, much of the Church is headed towards being a house of prayer. But in order for us to be a people upon whom the Lord can look, we need to be humble and broken before Him. The result will be that even as our plans and strategies can seem waylaid, we will learn to turn our failures and prisons into places of prayer and worship. We will begin to know that even when worst-case scenarios go down, God can and will glorify Himself. The battle is, in fact, the Lord's.

The Eleventh-hour Shaking

Back in Philippi, Paul and Silas, after being arrested, were beaten, locked up, and their feet were put in stocks. Often in the Bible, feet symbolize our ability to go forward with the gospel. Isaiah 52:7 reads, *"How lovely on the mountains are the feet of him who brings good news, who announces peace and brings good news of happiness, who announces salvation."* In the New Testament, Paul tells the Ephesian saints to *"shod your feet with the preparation of the gospel of peace"*

(Ephesians 6:15, NAS). In order for our feet to move with the gospel of peace out of the prisons of our safe and comfortable altars of orthodoxy, we definitely need a bigger revelation of God, His sovereignty, and especially His perfect love which casts out fear.

"About midnight Paul and Silas were praying and singing hymns of praise to God, and the prisoners were listening to them" (Acts 16:25, NAS). As we are entering into perhaps the "eleventh hour" of the Church Age, God is doing a new thing with prayer and worship. Not that what He is doing is new in scripture, but the depth of it is new to the body of Christ today.

The end-time Church will be a house of prayer. We are going to become a people who, not only in our theology but in our lives, learn to worship the Father in Spirit and in truth. As with Joshua before the battle of Jericho, we need a greater personal revelation of God's love and power. One that will put us on our faces before God in a listening mode so that we might learn to work out our salvation with fear and trembling (Phil. 2:12).

Again, as Paul and Silas were worshipping, the Lord shook the house down to its foundation, the doors were thrown open, and the chains were unfastened. The final outcome was so powerful that even the jailer and his whole family came to the Lord. This is the outpouring of the Spirit which is going to meet with the Church as we learn to worship the Father in Spirit and in truth.

What the Church and the world desperately need today is a sovereign shaking by God's presence. We do not need to be **raptured** so much as we need to be **recaptured** by **THE TRUTH**: that Jesus Christ is Lord of everything, even in the dirty now-and-now, and not just in the sweet by-and-by. The role of the Church is to be the scriptural people the Bible tells us to be: people of prayer and worship, people who obey every word that proceeds from the mouth of God.

The bottom line is that to obey is better than to make religious sacrifices. In fact, the real sacrifice the Lord desires is for us to become broken and humble before His throne, a people who delight in doing the Father's will. As with the people of Jesus' time, we desperately need a radical, root-level revelation of God to turn over the tables in the temple of our hearts. Because we are coming into a unique period in history, it is time for us to be still and listen. It will be a time God touches world cultures and populations to a deeper extent than the world has ever experienced. It will be to the extent that even many of the enemies of God's people will be saved, just like with the jailer of Paul and Silas.

> *I know that you can do all things: no plan of yours can be thwarted. Surely I spoke of things which I did not understand, things too wonderful for me to know. You said, 'Listen now, and I will speak: I will question you, and you shall answer me.' My ears had heard of you, but now my eyes have seen you. Therefore I despise myself and repent in dust and ashes.* (Job 42:1-6, NIV)

A Postscript

As a two-year postscript to the spring letter that comprised this chapter, I would like to relate the following story that happened at Foothills Christian Fellowship in El Cajon, CA (my home away from home church). It took place during the spring of 1994 when the church ran renewal meetings, Toronto style, for seven consecutive weeks.

In the midst of the renewal and the excitement around the outpouring of the Holy Spirit, one of the girls from the church invited her unsaved teenage friend who was suffering from anorexia. She was profoundly touched by the Holy Spirit that night and promptly surrendered her life to Jesus. Her parents, due to coming out of cult involvement, on hearing of her experience were furious and forbade her to attend any more meetings. But over the following few days the father noticed the absence of anger and rebellion in their daughter, and such a change in her personality and behavior that they agreed to accompany her to the Sunday a.m. service. After the service, they were invited home to one of the church family's for lunch. They then went back to the church for the p.m. service where the father was prayed for, and gave his life to Jesus. Within a few days at another renewal meeting, he was powerfully touched by the Holy Spirit. Over a period of the following few weeks, not only the mother, but the teenage son and a twelve-year-old son all gave their lives to Jesus. The marriage has been turned around, and the family as a whole is now living for Jesus and highly involved in the life of the church.

In this chapter, as I considered the incident of Paul and Silas worshipping God while firmly locked up in jail, I was reminded of this story out of El Cajon. Metaphorically speaking, in the renewal move of the last two years, the outpouring of the Holy Spirit has been shaking the Church just as God shook the jail in Philippi. God shook this church by the power of His presence and a small part of the fruit was that an entire family came to Jesus and entered into abundant life. As Haggai prophesied, *"This is what the LORD Almighty says: `In a little while I will once more shake the heavens and the earth, the sea and the dry land. I will shake all nations, and the desired of all nations will come, and I will fill this house with glory,' says the LORD Almighty"* (Haggai 2:6-7).

Let everything that can be shaken be shaken so that your glory reigns!

4fold

Power Authority

LION - Apostle

OX - Pastor Teacher
Shepherd

MAN - Evangelist
(unknown)

Eagle - Prophet

Set apart

Sons

High

Chapter Seven

Understanding the Role of
Prophetic Ministries Today

In Ezekiel 1 and Revelation 4, two different prophets describe similar visions of four beings representing worship and the will of God. One being had the face of a lion, the second an eagle, the third an ox, and the fourth was like a man. Among other things, the four beings depict the four-fold ministerial offices Paul mentions in Ephesians, chapter 4.

The ox is symbolic of the pastor/teacher: the steady worker whose success is not measured in bursts of power or glory, but in the day-in-day-out, steady, and patient plodding of a shepherd. The man portrays the evangelist; this is the office best able to relate the truths of God to those who do not know Him. The lion represents the apostle: power and authority in the jungle, so to speak, of one sent to release the King's order (It is no mistake many monarchies use the lion in their crests or emblems). Finally, the eagle figures the prophet: one slightly set apart, who soars in the highest places but also has the best vision to see what is happening a long way off.

As I said in the first chapter, we are entering into times Joel spoke of, when the Lord is touching all of humanity and is wanting His people to have eyes to see and ears to hear.

In the midst of God's raising up prophetic ministries in a new way, it is important to understand not only what the purpose of these ministries are but also what are their limitations.

You Shall All Know the Lord

Understanding the purpose and limitations of the prophetic is essential if the Church wishes to stabilize the typical pendulum reaction to prophecy - from Pharisaic fear to quick-fix thinking. Five basic but important distinctions between Old and New Testament prophetic ministries aid our understanding.

First is authority. The prophets in the Old Testament had tremendous authority, in varying degrees, because they were the only ones who could hear from the Lord on a regular basis. In contrast, today all Christians have anointing from the Holy Spirit to know God and to be led in a very personal Father/child relationship.

So the basic distinction between the old and new covenant has incredible ramifications regarding New Testament prophetic ministry. In Jeremiah 31:33-34 the Lord declares, *"...I will put my law in their minds and write it on their hearts. I will be their God, and they will be my people. No longer will a man teach his neighbor, or a man his brother, saying, 'Know the LORD,' because they will all know me, from the least of them to the greatest."* 1 John 2:27 (NIV) in a similar vein says, *"...the anointing you received from Him remains in you, and you do not need anyone to teach you. But as His anointing teaches you about all things and as that anointing is real, not counterfeit".*

The most crucial truth of the gospel is not only that a legal payment has been paid but that now we might also know God on a highly personal basis. Jesus did not come merely to give us free fire insurance, but He came to restore man to a relationship of intimacy with God.

Up to the resurrection, only a few select individuals actually had the Spirit of God in their lives. Those anointed by God were the prophets, judges, certain kings, and a few other people. And that anointing was not what we call "born again." The Spirit on them was often an anointing, or a capacity, to do the Lord's will. This was why, when confronted by Nathan the prophet for sinning with Bathsheba, David so ardently sought to retain the Spirit's anointing, according to David's prayer in Psalm 51.

Our anointing and intimacy with God does not take away the need for pastors, leaders, and teachers; nonetheless, as individuals our lives are to be directed by God and not man. One of the very basic scriptural examples of this principle is 2 Corinthians 9:7, *"Each man should give what he has decided in his heart to give, not reluctantly or under compulsion, for God loves a cheerful giver."* Many churches that abuse authority manipulate people concerning money. But the basic principle of the new covenant is that we are to be led by the Spirit as opposed to being controlled by man.

One classic biblical example of this is in Acts 21, when the respected prophet Agabus came to Paul with a prophetic warning of what would happen to him if he went to Jerusalem. The people who heard that prophecy attempted to persuade Paul to heed the prophecy and not go. But Paul reserved the right to be directed by the inner voice of God in his life. This did not subtract from the authenticity of Agabus' ministry; indeed, his word was fulfilled, but it meant Paul had to process that word through the grid of his own wisdom, experience, faith, and personal leading of the Holy Spirit.

1 Corinthians 14:3 (NIV) says prophecy is for the purpose of *"strengthening, encouragement, and comfort."* Nowhere in the New Testament does it say anything about prophecy's controlling, manipulating, or condemning anyone. "Directional" prophecies, either personal or corporate, must be worked through the framework of His children being led by the Spirit as individuals (see Romans 8:14).

Control Manipulate
Condemn

81

Obviously, leaders are called to lead, preach, teach, and sometimes rebuke - but when it comes to individual choice as to how, when, and where to serve God, we must recognize that is our priesthood, which Jesus died to give us.

Contemporary Prophecy Versus "Thus Sayeth the Lord"

The second difference between prophecy then and now also has to do with differences of delegated authority between logos and rhema. Today, because the Bible is complete, all prophecy is going to be rhema as opposed to logos. The general distinction between logos and rhema is that the inspired Logos was intended by God to not just have an effect on the people of that time, but to be eventually canonized into what we call the Bible - to have an impact on God's people throughout the ages.

Rhema is itself also inspired by the Holy Spirit, but it is meant only for a specific person or group, a specific situation, and a specific time. In other words, the difference between logos and rhema is the difference between general and specific truth.

Rhema not meant to be canonized as the Logos was also around in Old Testament times. Many Bible teachers today say the gift of prophecy does not exist now because the Bible is complete. That argument overlooks the full use of prophecy in the bible. There were often groups of prophets, such as the "Sons of the prophets" in Samuel, that obviously prophesied but their words were not meant to be canonized. Acts 11:27 and 13:1 talks about prophets, including Agabus, but we do not have any major messages from them - as we did from Samuel, Isaiah, or Jeremiah - intended as instruction for our lives.

Again, the question is not whether God actually speaks today, for He most certainly does. The point is God does not delegate authority in the same way to prophecies or to prophetic ministries as in Old Testament times.

In a seminar entitled "Developing the Prophetic Church: Learning to Converse with the Father", I encourage people not to preface prophetic words with "Thus sayeth the Lord." I believe that phrase implies a measure of authority the Holy Spirit does not intend. A word of rhema is to be prayed and thought through the individual's own priesthood rather than to be obeyed in blind obedience.

I sometimes refer to personal prophecy concerning future direction and goals as a "diving board into a pool of prayer.". As an individual seeks the Lord for confirmation, he or she is likely open to hearing things from the Lord which otherwise might not have been heard. Often, what the Lord in His goodness has prepared for our futures is either too good or too radically different for us to imagine. At this point, an outside word can open us up to new perspectives.

As 1 Corinthians 2:9 (NIV) says, *"No eye has seen, no ear has heard, no mind has conceived what God has prepared for those who love him."*

Mercy and Compassion Versus Wrath and Judgment

Another key difference in correctly handling prophecy today is understanding that through Christ, judgment has been paid. Jesus did not come to destroy but to bring abundant life. Often "wanna-be" prophets and individuals who actually do have prophetic gifting use as their role models prophets like Elijah and Jeremiah. The problem with this is such latter-day prophets fail to get the whole picture of their role model's hearts.

The classic example is James and John, the "sons of thunder," who wanted to call down fire from heaven to destroy a Samaritan village. Their model was Elijah when he called down fire from heaven to destroy two companies of soldiers. In righteous wrath and indignation, on behalf of Jesus, James and John wanted the people destroyed. Jesus replied to them, *"You do not know what kind of spirit you are of; for the Son of Man did not come to destroy men's lives, but to save them"* (Luke 9:54, NAS).

The point is clear: the Holy Spirit does not gift people in order to destroy. Some would say the Lord's taking Ananias and Saphira in Acts 5 disproves this, but there is no clear proof that when Peter confronted them He did it in front of the entire congregation. That the young men were outside the door when Peter spoke to Saphira suggests it was a small gathering. In any event, in that situation the lying to the Holy Spirit was serious enough that God did not allow any future chance of repentance, at least in this dimension.

Many times I hear of prophetic ministries that in public rebuke and condemn and speak out hidden sins. It is as if the prophetic office were a quick-fix operation for ailing churches. It is not enough to be able to see the truth, however, because Satan himself is constantly seeing our sins and accusing us before the throne of God. On the contrary, Isaiah 42 uses two phrases to describe a struggling believer, saying Jesus would not "break a bent reed" or blow out a "flickering wick".

For many who have come to Christ, these two phrases aptly identify them. To become whole is not a quick fix; for many it is learning to work out their salvation in fear and trembling, with a lot of love and acceptance and wisdom as part of the healing process.

When truth comes without love, the result is usually death and destruction. It was the Pharisees, who, with no love or compassion, dragged the woman caught in adultery in front of Jesus and the crowd (Matthew 8:3). Jesus, in speaking to her, said he did not condemn her.

Many times while I have been ministering, the Lord has pointed out to me sins and hypocrisy about people, but there are ways of dealing rebukes and warnings without destroying a person. It is Satan who brings condemnation to destroy. It is the Spirit of God who convicts, bringing encouragement unto repentance. As Psalm 85:10 (NAS) says, *"Lovingkindness and truth have met together; Righteousness and peace have kissed each other".*

Yes, God gives prophetic insight into hidden sins, but a prophet who only sees the truth but does not know the Father's heart can also be a false prophet because he is not truly representing the character of God.

God's Authority is Both Inherent and Delegated

Another problematic area for many churches and especially leaders is prophetic people who do not understand delegated authority. These are the wanna-be's who cloud themselves in cloaks of mysticism. They are above accountability to any pastor or church leader on the premise "they are hearing from God," and everyone needs to submit to their revelation. Implicit in their message is their special "pipe line" to God which renders them spiritually superior to basic Bible principles.

The point here is the difference between God's inherent authority and His delegated authority. In Old Testament times, prophets like Samuel and Elijah occasionally had more authority even than kings. But, as discussed earlier, there is a radical difference between God's delegated authority to prophets then and now.

Possibly the only parallel now to a prophet like Elijah would be the office of Apostle. Even there, biblical guidelines for relationship and accountability still apply.

If people are actually walking with God, they have proper regard, not only for what God is calling them to do, but they also have a respect for God's anointing and authority in others.

Obviously, Jesus had no sin to repent of, yet when He came to John the Baptist He submitted to John's prophetic call to be baptized according to Luke 3. Jesus respected the authority the Father had given John.

The principal of accountability and fellowship is firmly established in the New Testament. Hebrews 13:17 (NIV) reads, *"Obey your leaders and submit to their authority. They keep watch over you as men who must give an account. Obey them so that their work will be a joy, not a burden, for that would be of no advantage to you"*.

Many pseudo-prophets are in real sin. They lead a lifestyle of being belligerent and forceful in trying to usurp a pastor's or elder's authority. Part of the problem is that often God does gift some individuals in a fellowship to a greater degree of prophetic anointing than some of the leaders.

The situation can grow into a problem if one or two things are happening: (1) the leaders are insecure and are unable to receive any questions, or encouragement from the body; (2) those prophetically gifted are not honoring the authority God has given their leaders. James 3:17 (NIV) says, *"Wisdom that comes from heaven is first of all pure; then peace-loving, considerate, submissive, full of mercy and good fruit, impartial and sincere"*. He contrasts this with earthly wisdom which stems from envy and selfish ambition.

Much of the time, self-styled "prophets" cause headaches and division for leaders. These prophets perhaps see the truth in part, but they operate out of false ambition for power and control. The NAS translation of James 3:17, says wisdom from above is reasonable, meaning that it can be discussed and prayed through, as opposed to being manipulative and controlling.

Two of the main characteristics I look for in prophets, even more than accuracy, is humility of character and scriptural relationships with leaders in the body of Christ.

Accuracy and the Learning Curve

One main argument against prophetic gifting today is the claim no one today is absolutely perfect in all prophecies. My primary objection to that line of reason is that, in looking at the New Testament, I am not even sure the point is valid theologically. Jesus never said we would know a prophet by how accurate his prophecies would be, but, rather, a prophet can be tested by the fruit of his ministries (Matthew 7:15-16).

Paul, in 1 Corinthians 14 (NIV) says, *"Two or three prophets should speak, and the others should weigh carefully what is said"*. He does not say let two or three wanna-be's prophesy, but let two or three prophets prophesy. The inference is clear: there were people in the Church at that time who definitely had the gift of prophecy, but their words needed to be judged.

Basically, a prophetic word can come from one of three sources: (1) from the Holy Spirit; (2) from one's own imagination; or (3) the spiritual realm other than the Holy Spirit. ? (demonic)

For the average person to take risks and grow in knowing the difference between his own mind and the spiritual realm, it probably takes years, if not a lifetime. I am not implying God cannot speak clearly, but it can take the listening prophet years to unlearn the motives and confusion of the world.

And until that time, it can be easy for the "eyes and ears of our hearts" to taint or filter what we hear and see. With the gift of prophecy, like most of life, there is going to be a learning curve that will involve mistakes.

Several factors go into making up a check list for judging a prophecy: (1) Is it scriptural in theme? (2) Does it bring peace, even though it may call for a radical shift in focus? (3) Do two or more mature people bear witness with it? (4) Are people encouraged to draw closer to the Lord or is it just pseudo spiritual words?

The main thing I look for in a prophetic ministry is long-term fruit. Are people being encouraged to seek after the Lord? Are people going deeper into prayer, holiness, and obedience to the Lord? Is life coming forth as a result of that ministry? Jesus, in talking about knowing the Father's will, said to ask the Father for food (Luke 11:11-13). We could trust Him not to give us a snake, (symbolic for demonic deception).

Jesus also promised us the Holy Spirit would lead us and guide us into all truth (John 16:13). But just like every other area of life we enter in as beginners and like children learn to walk. Sometimes this involves making mistakes. The key is the motivation of our hearts. If we are honestly attempting to serve God, by His grace we will bear fruit in the long run, because He does want His children to be led by His Spirit (Romans 8:14).

Comfort, Strength, and Encouragement

Last, I see a change in priorities reflecting changes in the covenants and the outpouring of the Holy Spirit. I believe the main function of a prophetic ministry should be to reproduce itself. There is a parallel here with the office of evangelist. What an evangelist is to the unchurched the prophet should be to the Church. Evangelists who are current with the Holy Spirit will also put a strong emphasis on training ordinary Christians in evangelism. Likewise, prophetic ministries should also teach and train the body of Christ in the art of intimacy with God.

On a final note, the true function of a prophet is still the same as it was in the time of Samuel: to encourage God's people to draw closer to the heart of the Lord. In fact, the true prophet is one who is used by God to point out, with love and charity, the heart and throne of God. The difference today is that prophets and prophecy are given to encourage and build up individuals in their own priesthood, that we might truly be a nation of priests.

I, the LORD, have called you in righteousness; I will take hold of your hand. I will keep you and will make you to be a covenant for the people and a light for the Gentiles, to open eyes that are blind, to free captives from prison and to release from the dungeon those who sit in darkness.

I am the LORD; that is my name! I will not give my glory to another or my praise to idols. See, the former things have taken place, and new things I declare; before they spring into being I announce them to you (Isaiah 42:6-9, NIV).

The revelation of Jesus Christ, which God gave him to show his servants (Revelation 1:1, NIV).

Chapter Eight

The Year of the Lion

Everyone who has surrendered his or her life to the Lord Jesus has experienced a revelation of the lamb of God. Much of the Church, seemingly, has not really experienced a revelation Jesus' other side - that is the Lion of the tribe of Judah.

For many Christians, much of the battle between "salvation" Christianity (where the focus is on being saved) and "lordship" Christianity (where the focus is on being a disciple) has to do with lack of revelation. A lack of revelation stems from a lack of basic intimacy with God. This results in partial heart knowledge, or spiritual knowledge, of who Christ is. It follows, then, that ministry suffers, for it is out of the heart rather than the head that life and real ministry flows. Jesus said, *"The good man brings good things out of the good stored up in his heart"* (Luke 6:14, NIV).

At the close of each year, I typically spend the last few weeks seeking the Lord's overriding theme for my messages in the coming year. In December of 1993, without receiving full insight, the Lord drew my focus to Amos 3:8, which says, *"The lion has roared - who will fear? The Sovereign LORD has spoken - who can but prophesy?"*

As 1994 unfolded - with the Holy Spirit's outpouring in Toronto and many other areas in the Western world, especially North America and England - the Lord clarified His message. At the Airport Vineyard Christian Fellowship in Toronto since January of that year, thousands of Christians from all over the globe have been touched significantly by the Holy Spirit.

A conservative estimate is that somewhere in excess of 100,000 people from January, 1994, to January, 1995 - many of whom have come from other countries and even continents - have come to Toronto and encountered the Lord in a life-changing way. More than 10,000 pastors from all over North America, Europe, and other continents have come and experienced both refreshment (Acts 3:19) and new impartations of gifts and power from the Lord.

It would be incorrect to label this phenomenon as "revival," because true revival involves great numbers of first-time conversions. Nevertheless, we are confident the current move of the Holy Spirit is part of His preparation for major revival in the Church.

The present outpouring is affecting the Church in two primary ways. First, those who are weary are being refreshed. Second, those who are in varying stages of a "prodigal" condition are coming home to a party the Father is throwing.

At the same time as the Toronto outpouring, countless similar outbreaks of the Holy Spirit are occurring in churches and multi-church gatherings across North America. It seems, however, that Toronto, is one of the major "wellsprings".

This is partial fulfillment of a four-page, two-part prophecy, I received from the Lord in May, 1992 and June, 1993, concerning Toronto. Very simply, the vision was of living waters like Niagara Falls coming over the city and flowing like a mighty river eastward across Canada, and then going to the nations. Because of what God is doing, it behooves us to discover His goal and what He wants to release to His people this year.

A Prophetic Renewal of Worship

I Kings 13 illustrates what the Lord is doing. It describes a basic tale of conflict between the Holy Spirit and Pharisaism, wrongful motives, and tradition. It begins with a prophet coming to Bethel ("house of the Lord", in Hebrew) from Judah. The word Judah means "praise," but the connotations go even deeper. First, one confesses God's attributes; second, in the light or revelation of who God truly is, one confesses his or her shortcomings and weaknesses.

A major part of the prophetic restoration God has for His people today is a renewal of true worship. As our worship is renewed, we learn to wait on His Spirit and respond to Him instead of merely going through the motions. We learn by revelation that God is the Great I Am, and we are the great were not!

One element of the Toronto meetings - and other cities, as well - which speaks to me is not the power, laughter, or the manifestations, but the worship. People's hunger for God, coming together night after night and sometimes worshipping for an hour or more, is, I believe, a true sign of the renewal God wants to bring to His bride - a return to our first love.

Worship, along with prayer, is not only the battle ground in the 90's, but it is the meeting place from which God will send His people out to do battle. Judges 1:2 reads, *"The LORD answered, "Judah is to go; I have given the land into their hands."* Judges 20:18 similarly says, *"The Israelites went up to Bethel and inquired of God. They said, "Who of us shall go first to fight against the Benjamites?" The LORD replied, "Judah shall go first."*

The second passage concerns Israel's bringing restoration to the Hebrew people. In the same way today, God wants to release His heart and passion into His people in order to free us of complacency, fear, and unbelief within ourselves so we can go after the enemy without.

In I Kings 13, the king who resisted a prophetic message is an exact picture of many leaders today who

93

have made an idol out of order and control, and insist their traditions and methods in ministry are the only way.

In such churches, concern for healing people and setting them free can be secondary to maintaining the program. Too many leaders are far more concerned with protecting **their** empire instead of seeking the kingdom of God and being right with Him.

As the prophet rebuked the false worship, the king stretched out his hand and gave orders to seize him. But as he did so, his arm and hand completely withered to the point that he was unable to withdraw it.

This is a crucial lesson leaders must learn. The Holy Spirit can be grieved, and, in a time when He is pouring out revelation of the Father's heart and glory, if leaders respond in an attitude of criticism, trying to keep a hold of their own empires and traditions, judgment will be released. Attitudes and the characteristics of Pharisaism, such as critical hearts, lack of mercy, and legalism will begin to overwhelmingly dominate them. In short, God will partially give them over to one of the chief sins a Christian can commit: grieving the Holy Spirit.

One thing God hates, according to Proverbs 6:19 (NIV), is *"a man who stirs up dissension among brothers"*. In the "true fast" of Isaiah 58, God warns to put away the pointing of the finger. Like the king in the story, many leaders who Pharisaically attack the Spirit's work will end up increasingly devoid of love and humility.

As Paul states in II Corinthians 3:6 (NIV), we are to be ministers "not of the letter but of the Spirit; for the letter kills, but the Spirit gives life." Just as the king's condition was evident to all in I Kings 13, if God, out of a grieved heart, removes part of His grace from some ministries, those leaders' true motives will be exposed. As the old fable goes, everyone will know that the "king is naked."

94

Malachi 3:18 (NIV) reads, *"You will again see the distinction between those who serve God and those who do not."* In I Kings, the king quickly repented, the prophet prayed for him, and the king was healed. The king then offered the prophet a reward, but the prophet replied the Lord had told him to go home without even eating or drinking, and to return by a different route. As Elisha once asked his servant, *"Is this the time to take money, or to accept clothes, olive groves, vineyards, flocks, herds, or menservants and maidservants?"*

This is a lesson for those who would respond today: we must not let our hearts become filled with pride and attitudes of elitism but we must receive God's heart for the whole body of Christ.

An Hour has Come

The book of John presents a picture of the discipleship times we are in. Jesus said, in John 12:23, the hour had come for the Son of Man to be glorified. He then began to speak of dying to one's self and being like seed that is buried in the ground but then bears fruit. He ended by stating He was contemplating the cost the Father was calling Him to make. John 12:27 (NIV) quotes Jesus as saying, "My heart is troubled".

There are two key points here for us today. One, we are, so to speak, in the eleventh hour of history. And this is a time when, as the prophet Joel stated, the Spirit of God is going to be touching all of mankind (Joel 2:28). But to enter into Jesus' sort of discipleship, we are going to have to die to our own agendas and goals.

Two, if Jesus' soul was troubled by the price tag He paid to be obedient to the Father, it will certainly be a troubling cost you and I will have to pay. Nonetheless, this is what God is looking for, at a time when He pursuing the nations - people who are so radically in love with Him they are willing to die for Him.

Continuing the account in I Kings 13, the prophet on his way home was greeted by an older prophet who told him it was okay with God if he came home with him and ate a meal. So the younger prophet went with the elder. But even as they were at table, the older prophet, by the Spirit of the Lord, rebuked the younger for failing to carry out the whole word of the Lord.

The younger prophet went on his way, but a lion came out of the wilderness and killed him. On hearing this, the older prophet went after him and found him dead in the road. Interestingly, the dead man had been neither eaten nor mauled by the lion. Moreover, sitting by the body was both the lion and the prophet's unafraid donkey. Obviously, this was no ordinary lion; this is a picture of the lion of the tribe of Judah.

This may sound like a harsh Old Testament story to Christians today, but I believe this vividly depicts God's jealousy over those to whom He gives revelation of Himself (see James 4:5).

We are in a major time of God's Spirit moving on the nations. In the coming years, God will radically call His people to have an abandonment in seeking Him and His will. He will call many into missions and evangelism. In fact, He will call many of us into radical evangelism.

Already, we have seen two or three remarkable miracles take place here in Toronto by the Lord's using young girls who have never ministered in healing before. This is a sign of what is to come. It is going to be the average Christian who responds to the call of the Lion and is going to be the initial giant killer.

But to whom much is given, much is required. In the outpouring of God's Spirit, the real revelation is not so much about dates and events as it is of God himself. And just as the prophet was killed by the lion, those who respond to God will be called into accountability for what we do with the revelation of God.

This move of the Spirit in the nineties is not just a charismatic or Pentecostal experience concerning power or gifting. It is one thing to be clothed with power, but it is another to be indwelt with the person of God. In the ministry times in Toronto, we have been encouraging people not just to get the experience but to soak in the presence of the Lord.

Where is the Fruit?

Matthew 21 is a very important chapter in understanding end-time restoration, because it covers Jesus' final trip to Jerusalem. We are, in fact, in a time frame today when Jesus' Spirit wants to overturn the tables of church life and turn us into a house of prayer. I am convinced that if we truly want to see a powerful move of the Holy Spirit in the Western world, it will not happen until we learn to seek His face.

But what I would like to look at here are verses 17-20. Jesus, after the temple, the miracles, and the worship of the children, went to Bethany to spend the night. "Bethany," in the Hebrew, means "house of figs." Figs signified peace and prosperity. The juice of figs was also used on occasion for medicinal purposes. The fig tree is unusual in that unlike most fruit trees the fruit itself precedes the leaf. So Jesus, seeing the leaves, walked up to the tree and expected to find fruit. In His disappointment, He then cursed the fig tree, which rapidly withered.

Jesus said of the Father, in John 15:2 (NIV), *"He cuts off every branch in me that bears no fruit, while every branch that does bear fruit he prunes so that it will be even more fruitful"*. Many churches are like fig trees with leaves - having all the promise but no real nourishment for those who are thirsty and hungry. I believe God will soon increase judgment on churches and ministries that have all the programs and talk but

97

fail to bear the fruit: seeing lives healed and being transformed by His Spirit.

As Jeremiah rebuked the leaders in Jeremiah 6:14 and 8:14 (NIV), *"They dress the wound of my people as though it were not serious. "Peace, peace," they say, when there is no peace".* At a time when God is going forth like a mighty warrior, with a shout against His enemies (see Isaiah 42:13), He is taking very seriously leaders who are more concerned with maintaining the status quo and protecting their positions and reputations than in calling out to Him, "Not my will, but yours, Father ...whatever the cost".

When the Lion Roars

In numerous meetings since mid-1994, some people have been literally roaring as lions as the Spirit of God comes on them. Such unusual behavior is particularly difficult for the natural and/or the religious mind to put into perspective, since the manifestation is somewhat similar to that seen in demonized people. The difference, however, is these people exhibit no demonic anger or agony. Instead, a boldness and jealousy for God is in evidence. I believe this boldness is a prophetic manifestation of the fierceness in which the Lord is pursuing the lost and hurting.

Like everything else God does, people's flesh often tries to imitate it, and Satan tries to counterfeit it. This is where spiritual discernment is specifically needed.

It seems the roaring mainly comes on those who have multi-church ministries, church leaders, evangelists, or intercessors. No doubt this manifestation causes a wide array of reaction and criticism, but, as I see it, these are the Father's children imitating by the Holy Spirit what the Lord is doing in the heavenlies.

One of the criticisms will be a typical Pharisaic line: "I've never seen this before, so it can't be of God". One would think we want our Lion of Judah to be predictable and tame! To quote the characters in C.S. Lewis's *Chronicles of Narnia* whenever Aslan the lion (a Jesus figure) would unexpectedly appear and do unpredictable things, "Well, he's not really a tame lion, you know".

This, in essence, is the revelation the bride of Christ needs today. Our Savior, the Lamb of God, is also the Lion of the tribe of Judah, the King of Kings and Lord of Lords. He is not a God we can completely understand or completely be comfortable with. Our comfort is to come from the Holy Comforter, but that flows out of relationship with Him, not by us trying to be in control of our situation.

The contemporary Church needs to understand there are more promises in the Bible for those who fear God than there are for those who love Him. This does not detract from the fact that God is love and He always deals with His children in love. Even so, God does not deal with us only in love but also in truth. Psalm 85:10 (NIV) says, *"Love and faithfulness meet together; righteousness and peace kiss each other".* Just as truth without love is deadly, so love without the truth is a false or shallow love.

The Father seeks those who will worship in Spirit and in truth. The fruit of what the Spirit is currently doing is, as Philippians 2:12-13 (NIV) says, peoples' willingness to work out their *"salvation with fear and trembling; for it is God who works in you, both to will and to act according to His good purpose".* We need a revelation that God is not the great "I WAS," or the "I WILL BE", but right here, right now, He is the great I AM.

The Best is for Last

Throughout much of the Bible is this lesson: the best is often for last. Examples include Haggai's prophecy that the latter glory would be greater than the former,

99

Jesus' first miracle where He created at the end of a wedding party wine that was much better than what was served first, and Abraham's and Sarah's having promises from God fulfilled at a time when they thought old age had rendered the promises dead.

In Revelation 1, the apostle John, who in his life seemingly saw everything there is to see this side of heaven, came into probably the greatest revelation of Jesus as Lord of the Church that anyone had ever experienced. After years of seeing the gospel touch most of the known world, after seeing the Mount of Transfiguration, the Ascension, and all the miracles of Jesus, as well as what He and the other disciples had done, John was imprisoned on the Island of Patmos.

Much of the church in the West today has an "island" mentality which keeps us locked up. We are afraid to go out and touch our neighborhoods and workplaces with the reality of God's love. While there is so much fear in the Church of the antichrist, the new age movement, cults, etc., I believe the biggest revelation of Jesus and His glory touching the world will come in these last days.

Isaiah 42:13 and 16 (NIV) says, (13) *"The Lord will march out like a mighty man, like a warrior He will stir up His zeal; with a shout he will raise the battle cry and will triumph over his enemies. (16) I will lead the blind by ways they have not known, along unfamiliar paths I will guide them; I will turn the darkness into light before them and make the rough places smooth. These are the things I will do; I will not forsake them"*.

Chapter Nine

The Nineties in Perspective

Poised at the mid-point of the nineties, January, 1995, I would like to relate four words (or visions) concerning churches in the Western world, Japan, Great Britain, and Germany. The first is a general word of encouragement for churches that have made a priority of seeking the Lord and being obedient to the leading of His Spirit, rather than being controlled by methodology or tradition. The succeeding three words are specifically for churches in Great Britain, Germany, and Japan, respectively. The time frame for these last three visions was approximately eighteen to twenty-four months, beginning mid `94 for England and January 1, 1995, for Japan and Germany.

Birth Pangs

Contained both in the Bible and in contemporary prophecies is the promise of a major move of God. This will be a move which, in both scope and power, will surpass any the Church has ever seen. It will be the fulfillment of Joel's promise of a time when the Spirit would be poured out on all of mankind (Joel 2:28), of Haggai's prophecy of a second time when God would shake the nations (Haggai 2:7), of Jesus' prophecy that His believers would do even "greater works" than what He had done (John 14:12), of His prophetic prayer to the Father in John 17:17-23 that the Church would be perfected in unity, and of Jesus' prophecy in Matthew 24 that the time would come when the gospel would be preached to all nations, or ethnic groups (Matthew 24:14).

Several, if not all these passages, seem to point to an end-time move of the Holy Spirit. For example, Joel's prophecy was interpreted by Peter on the day of Pentecost as being a last-days' event. If, as Peter believed, the last days began almost 2,000 years ago, how much more are we truly in the last days of the last days?

Some would argue the "greater works" prophecy has already been fulfilled in the ministries of men like Billy Graham. But the words Jesus used in John 14 for "greater works" - the same as He used in John 5:20 - specifically refer to miraculous works. Although healings and miracles are on the increase, the time has not yet come when believers are performing "greater works." Neither has the time arrived when the body of Christ is truly united around what the Spirit is saying and doing.

In the last twenty years or so, God has used many key voices to speak prophetically to the body of Christ. These point to an incredible end-time move of the Lord's Spirit. So that we might recognize this movement, we can identify three chief characteristics.

First, from all nations, a massive flood of people will come to Christ. It is safe to say, in looking at Joel 2:28, this end-time move of the Spirit will make the same basic impact on every neighborhood, city, school, and workplace as Jesus and His disciples did for three-and-a-half years throughout the nation of Israel. Before the Lord's return, every individual will be confronted by the kingdom of God in such a way as to be forced to make a conscious decision concerning Jesus. As at the trial of Jesus, either people will be disciples or they will be adamantly against Him. Only this time it will be the world on trial and Jesus will be the judge.

Second, this end-time move of God's Spirit will be a demonstration not only of God's sovereignty and power but also of His incredible compassion. The promise of John 14:12 will be fulfilled, with miracles, signs, and wonders becoming commonplace. Blind eyes seeing, the lame walking, the deaf hearing, etc. will be more the norm than the exception as the gospel begins to powerfully touch the lost and hurting.

This is already true in a few areas such as Nagaland, India, where healings are already a way of life rather than being anomalies. The main problem I see in the cessationist's argument (which holds that because the Bible is canonized and the first Apostles are gone, healings, signs, and wonders have ceased) is that God is the same yesterday, today, and forever. He is the same God now who healed then out of compassion for the lost and hurting (Matthew 20.32-34). There has never been a time in church history when healing has ever ceased, especially in diseased and exhaustion-ridden areas of the world.

Our God will be moving in great power through His disciples. It will be in this end-time move that John 14:12 will be fulfilled.

In keeping with Joel's promise of a prophetic time for men and women, young and old, I believe John 14:12 will be experienced by much of the end-time Church, regardless of denomination. This will not be a movement for just a few superstars. Already in Toronto, teenagers who have never moved in the Spirit before have been touched by the renewal. Amazingly, they are beginning to move in strong healings and evangelism.

Last, many churches will see their denominational walls break down. That is not to say churches will lose their uniqueness. On the contrary, just as Elijah built the alter on Mount Carmel with twelve stones, one for each of the twelve tribes, the end-time move of God will be made up of churches unique in their God-given distinctions.

For the purpose of taking cities for Christ, churches will come together for prayer and worship in a unity centered around the leading of the Holy Spirit. As leaders begin to get a bigger revelation of God's glory and holiness, we will begin to understand our uniqueness can be no cause for pride or walls, but, rather, we will begin to get the Father's heart for one another. It is only in unity that our uniqueness can come together to complement one another.

The time is drawing near - and, in fact, is already here for some cities - for churches to come together and fill arenas and halls with prayer and worship.

Bringing in the First Fruits

The real move of the end-time harvest is still some eight to ten years away for most cities in the Western world. As in the time of John the Baptist, we are going through a period of prophetic restoration of our hearts and lives in preparation for the move of the Lamb of God.

Interestingly, many churches, unable to get enough volunteers for their own Sunday school programs, feel ready to reap an end-time harvest. For them, the perspective of "If you can't do it in Jerusalem, you're not ready for Samaria" is good to keep in mind.

Many of us need to be recaptured by God's love. We need to return to a place of abandonment in our hearts to God's will and purposes.

But those seriously seeking first the kingdom of God and responding to the Holy Spirit are, metaphorically speaking, already immersed in the Jordan. Historically, entering into the Jordan symbolizes two truths: change or repentance, as with John the Baptist's ministry, and entering into the promises of God, as with the Hebrews crossing the Jordan.

In general, like the River of Life described in Ezekiel 47, the current move of the Holy Spirit (what some call the "Toronto Blessing") is the River of Life at the ankle level - bringing spiritual refreshment. This is not to say there is any sort of elite group of people, such as those who have traveled to Toronto, or those who have been touched by the manifestations. The Holy Spirit moves and speaks through a myriad of ways. No matter His method, God is speaking, refreshing, and anointing many right now. It is critical that we respond to Him in His perfect timing, regardless of how He chooses to speak.

The first level of the River of Life was only ankle deep. That may not seem like much compared to the fourth and final stage, where Ezekiel could not ford the river because of the strength and depth of the water. Nonetheless, the feet, covered by ankle-deep water, are symbolic of taking forward the good news (see Isaiah 52:7, Luke 9:5, and Ephesians 6:15).

The twelve spies who initially crossed into the promised land brought back not only a report of what they saw and experienced but they also brought back tangible evidence. Numbers 13:23 (NIV) reads, *"When they reached the Valley of Eshcol, they cut off a branch bearing a single cluster of grapes. Two of them carried it on a pole between them, along with some pomegranates and figs."*

In like manner, I believe many who respond to the Spirit of God and get wet in the now-flowing river of Life will have a new freedom and anointing throughout the decade; they will be the ones to bring back the first fruits. Even though we are still several years away from the culturally transforming renewals, such as some third-world countries are experiencing, the first fruits are now going to become visible, and, as with the twelve spies, they will come in heavy bunches.

Without wanting to go into more detail at this point, I will say that everything the Lord has been speaking to me concerning the decade of the nineties has to do with God's mercy and compassion towards hurting and desperate people who do not really know Him at this time.

A Word for the British Isles
(First publicly released in London, June, 1994)

I believe this is a word for the Anglicans of Great Britain and also for the larger Body of Christ in the British Isles.

The Lord showed me vision of a large traditional church building. It could have been anywhere in Great Britain. The walls were of stone and natural-colored brick, and it had a slate roof. Tremendous winds began to blow ferociously against the church.

[As an aside, it is important to keep in mind that the word for "Spirit" in the Hebrew is the word "ruwach" which means "wind" or "breath;" it can also mean a "violent exhalation." In Acts 2:2, prior to the disciples' preaching of the gospel to the city of Jerusalem, the Holy Spirit came over the twelve as a "mighty, rushing wind." This was clearly a different experience than John 20:22, when Jesus first breathed on the disciples.]

As the winds reached their heaviest, the four walls of the church building were completely blown away to the point one could not even see any debris. Despite the building's collapse, the hand of the Lord held up the roof, which did not move. The four missing walls of brick began to be replaced by glass walls which were strong enough to support the roof, but were completely transparent.

As this transition was taking place, two things happened. One, the people inside the church began to see quite clearly the people outside. That is to say, they began to see the world though the eyes of God. Many people in the church who had never had a burden for the lost and hurting began to go out and minister God's love to those outside, and bring them into the Kingdom of God.

At the same time, people outside the church, such as passersby and church neighbors, began to see into the church and see the reality of God among His people. Most of these people had avoided the church in the past because they assumed Christians were just "quaint, religious people" who were out of touch with reality. I believe the Lord showed me He had begun in 1995 a process of renewal in many churches throughout Great Britain, and was preparing them for the work of the harvest.

A Word for Japan
(First released publicly in September, 1994)

In another vision, I saw tremendous winds and waves - Tsunami storms - hitting the nation of Japan. I believe the Lord was showing me the nation was going to be shaken economically, politically, physically, and even spiritually. The period of the winds and waves hitting the Islands was approximately eighteen months.

I saw an increase in political scandals and the yen plunging into deeper problems. The one overwhelming message the Lord gave me for Japan was that God loves the Japanese too much to leave them as they are; the only thing that would wake them up from idolatry of money and pride was a national shaking on all fronts. I even saw the nation being shaken geographically with mighty winds, waves, and earthquakes.

One week after I first saw this vision, in the early autumn, the news reported a huge storm in Japan which had killed a dozen people or so.

I believe the fruits of this overall storm of eighteen months will be in two areas. One, the churches and Christians actively seeking the Lord for their nation will experience a tremendous move as in the day of

Pentecost. There will be a new boldness with many Christians to step past cultural barriers and talk to fellow Japanese about Jesus. Also, there will be a greater freedom in some of the churches for healings and miracles to take place.

Second, because of these natural disasters, many Japanese who have been closed to Jesus because of pride, false religion, and materialism will be shaken and afraid for the future. They will begin to be more open to the gospel and will respond.

The world will take notice when this happens, for Japan has been notoriously difficult for the gospel to penetrate.

Editor's Note: Since the date of this prophecy, Japan has experience a major earthquake (killing over 4,000 people), and cultic terrorist activity that caused death and chaos on Japan's subway systems due to a highly lethal, poisonous gas. Further, confidence in Japan's once powerful economic structure has been mightily shaken, despite the strong Yen against the dollar.

A Word for Germany
(First released in December, 1994)

In the third vision, I saw vast fields of wheat ripe for the harvest. Gentle summer breezes of God's Spirit continually blew, causing the wheat to be flexible and move according to the direction of the wind. The summer sun beautifully shone on the fields.

Not a lot, perhaps ten percent, of the workers needed were out beginning to work the fields. But there was such a joy on these workers, that even though they were few in number, they were singing, dancing, and celebrating the work and harvest as they went about it. This joy they experienced in the Spirit of the Lord gave them great strength to do the work. Like the Gadites who chose to fight with David, "the least was a match for a hundred, and the greatest for a thousand."

Provoked by Jealousy

In the account of Gideon's initial victory against the Midianites and the Amalekites, God started with just three hundred men against possibly sixty thousand or more. Just the camels of the Midianites and the Amalekites *"could no more be counted than the sand on the seashore"* (Judges 7:12, NIV). The enemy soldiers were as "thick as locusts." When Gideon first began to have success, three other tribes, the Naphtali, Asher, and Manasseh were quick to join in. Then one of the leading tribes, Ephraim, also joined and was used by the Lord powerfully.

These other tribes were provoked by jealousy in joining in with what the Lord was doing. Even as a little bit of salt makes the whole salty, so a few churches entering into the first fruits will, in a healthy way, provoke other churches and leaders into entering in. This is a good jealousy, rather than a carnal one. It is a hunger which leads us to God's will and breaks pride and complacency.

Year of Jubilee

1995 marks the fiftieth anniversary of the end of World War II. There have been many prophetic words concerning the obvious jubilee-year comparison, especially for Germany. The jubilee year was time for slaves to be given freedom and debts to be canceled. The analogy for Germany, England, and Japan, is quite strong. These nations were not only three of the principal players involved in the fighting, but they were also devastated by the war.

The time is here, not only for cancellation of debts, as Christians intercede and ask forgiveness, but for renewal. This, in fact, has already begun in many churches; the first fruits of revival are ripening in the world's cultures.

In describing my vision of the harvest workers in Germany, I mentioned the Gadite warriors who were joining in with David. I Chronicles 12:8 (NIV) states, *"Their faces were the faces of lions."* This is symbolic of the warriors who are going to be in the forefront of God's army. They will be those who have experienced a revelation of Jesus as not only the Lamb of God but also as the Lion of the tribe of Judah.

Concerning these Gadite warriors, I Chronicles 12:15 (NIV) also says, *"It was they who crossed the Jordan in the first month when it was overflowing all its banks, and they put to flight everyone living in the valleys, to the east and to the west."* Just as John was baptizing people in preparation for the coming of the Lamb of God, the outpouring which began in 1993 to 1994 is also a baptism into the River of Life (which is mentioned in Ezekiel 47 and Revelation 22). Those who respond to the current outpouring of the Holy Spirit before any more time elapses are going to be in the forefront of the workers of the coming harvest.

May God arise, may his enemies be scattered; may his foes flee before him. As smoke is blown away by the wind, may you blow them away; as wax melts before the fire, may the wicked perish before God. But may the righteous be glad and rejoice before God; may they be happy and joyful. Sing to God, sing praise to his name, extol him who rides on the clouds - his name is the LORD - and rejoice before him. A father to the fatherless, a defender of widows, is God in his holy dwelling. God sets the lonely in families, he leads forth the prisoners with singing; but the rebellious live in a parched land. When you went out before your people, O God, when you marched through the wasteland, the earth shook, the heavens poured down rain, before God, the One of Sinai, before God, the God of Israel. You gave abundant showers, O God; you refreshed your weary inheritance. Your people settled in it, and from your bounty, O God, you provided for the poor. The Lord announced the word, and great was the company of those who proclaimed it. (Psalm 68:1-11, NIV)

Final Note

Again, I am not speaking of an elite group who have been to the Toronto Airport Vineyard Church or anywhere else in particular. Neither am I referring to those who may have experienced a manifestation. I am speaking of those who are crying out to God, laying down their lives, and praying, "Father, your will, not mine."

Appendix

A Brief, Biblical Look at Five Manifestations of the Holy Spirit

by Dave Hoffman and Marc DuPont

In February of 1994, the Lord Jesus poured out His Holy Spirit upon Foothills Christian Fellowship, a non-denominational, charismatic church in Southern California. Over a seven-week period, the church held extended evening meetings five nights a week. Many became Christians, while others recommitted their lives to Christ, had bondages broken, experienced emotional and physical healings, or simply were spiritually renewed in their lives.

During this outpouring, five distinguishing manifestations of the Holy Spirit as He ministered to individuals were noted. Many people asked, "Why all the shaking, laughing, weeping, and falling over? I just don't understand it! Is there Biblical support for what we see taking place?"

The following is a biblical response to these questions, prepared by Foothills' Pastor Dave Hoffman and edited by myself.

Balanced Discernment:
Bible knowledge, spiritual discernment, and knowing a little church history.

I do not believe we can ever provide unquestionable, biblical proof texts to support what God has been doing. For example, you will not find a scripture that says, "As we prayed for them, their bodies began to shake and some fell over. Go, and do likewise."

As I studied this matter, it became apparent that all the manifestations we are experiencing are mentioned in the Bible. Are these manifestations biblical? I would have to say an emphatic "Yes!" Are there specific proof texts for each manifestation? My response? "No!"

Much of what we consider good discernment is dependent on not only having a good knowledge of the Bible, but a close relationship with the Holy Spirit. Jesus said in the gospel of John that *"The Holy Spirit would lead us and guide us into all truth, and speak of the things yet to come."* Proverbs 3:5 says to lean not to our own understanding but to trust in the Lord with all of our hearts.

In Corinthians, Paul warns that the natural mind cannot understand or apprehend the things of the Spirit. At the same time, it is valid to ask theological questions and to pursue knowledge of the truth, as long as we keep in mind there is a difference between knowing about the truth and actually knowing the Truth Himself, who will truly lead us, guide us, and give us discernment.

It should be noted that in past outpourings and revivals in America, there have been varied physical manifestations. Jonathan Edwards was perhaps the most outstanding theologian in American history, greatly used by God in the "Great Awakening" (a powerful revival during 1740-1745). In *Account of Revival of Religion in Northampton, 1740-1742*, he writes about the effect of God's Spirit upon people: *"It was a very frequent thing to see outcries, faintings, convulsions and such like, both with distress and also admiration and joy."*

Though manifestations often accompany the Spirit's outpouring, we should also remember that our emphasis must not be on outward signs but the internal work of the Holy Spirit. Many who have come for prayer have exhibited no outward manifestation at all, but experienced tremendous touches from our Lord Jesus.

The Manifestations:

1) Trembling or Shaking

A host of scriptures in the Bible speak about individuals' trembling or shaking out of fear, awe, or terror. But we need to understand that in many of these passages the shaking is an involuntary reaction to the overwhelming, manifest presence - as opposed to the omnipresence - of the Lord. Many passages speak about the heavens or earth trembling, whole armies shaking, nations, trees shaking, and so forth, but for our purposes, let us start with Jeremiah:

Do you not fear me?" declares the Lord. "Do you not tremble in my presence?" (Jeremiah 5:22).

Here God seems to indicate His people will tremble when in His manifest presence.

"Worship the Lord with reverence and rejoice with trembling" (Psalm 2:11).

Here God seems to indicate that possibly while worshipping Him one can be overcome by His manifest presence.

Respectable individuals sometimes experienced, according to the scriptures, trembling when they heard words from the Lord or came into His manifest presence:

"When I heard, my inward parts trembled. At the sound my lips quivered... and in my place I tremble" (Habakkuk 3:16).

115

In Acts, we are told that Moses *"shook in the presence of the Lord"* (Acts 7:32).

Daniel trembled on his hands and knees when God touched him, and when he stood up he was still trembling, according to his own account in Daniel 10:8-10.

Scriptural evidence, then, supports the possibility of God's power being so great as to override our faculties to the point of causing our trembling or shaking when we encounter the manifest presence of God.

Some still object to the shaking, saying, "I don't understand it, it serves no purpose."

To those I would say, "Since when did man's understanding determine what God would do?" Just think of the cross - no one understood it. Do you think any of Jesus' followers saw God's hand in the arrest and crucifixion of Jesus before His resurrection? Our intellectual understanding should never be used as the sole criteria for determining what is of God.

I have heard others say, "Why would God manifest Himself in such a way as to scare people off, this just doesn't feel like God! God is a God of order not of confusion!" My dear reader, manifestations of God scare people simply because they are from God.

Many have decided for themselves what God can and cannot do, because they are comfortable with their designated parameters for God. They really do not want a God who is in control and sovereign. They want to have control so they draw back from sovereign demonstrations of God. Simply put, if God's presence causes a person to tremble and shake, then we should bless it!

2) Falling Over or "Slain in the Spirit"

I like what one man said when asked why individuals fall over when the Holy Spirit comes upon them. He said, "People fall over simply because they cannot stand up!" Or as one theologian has put it, "I did not so much fall down, but as the Lord's presence came over me, up came the floor!"

We have observed over the last months that when God's power overcomes some people, they fall to the ground and occasionally are unable to get up for long periods of time. Such examples can also be found in the Bible.

We are told in Chronicles that the priests "could not stand to minister" because God's presence filled the temple (II Chronicles 5:4 & I Kings 8:11). The word "stand" in Hebrew is "Amad" and means to stand up. If they could not stand, what was happening to them? I believe they were falling over because God's power enveloped them.

Many scriptures seem to indicate that when experiencing the Lord's presence or hearing His voice, individuals fall down:

Genesis 17:3	Leviticus 9:24
Numbers 16:45	Joshua 5:14
Judges 13:20	I Kings 18:29
I Chronicles 21:16	II Chronicles 20:18
Daniel 8:17	Daniel 10:8-10
Matthew 17:6	Revelation 1:17
Revelation 4:10	Revelation 7:11
Revelation 11:16	Revelation 22:8

Some may argue that these individuals who fell on their faces before God or after hearing His voice were merely doing so out of respect and awe, or simply because they were terrified. This may be true for many of the scriptures but not for all of them, especially when you look at passages like II Chronicles 5:4 or Daniel 10:8-10, for instance. Ezekiel, the prophet, fell over several times in the presence of God (Ezekiel 1:28,

,.23). Ezekiel 44:4 reads: *"I looked and saw the glory of the LORD filling the temple of the LORD, and I fell face down."* If you have ever been in a church meeting where someone literally falls face down, as Ezekiel describes, you can be sure it was not done on purpose, because if it were not caused by the Holy Spirit it would seriously damage the individual.

The Hebrew word for "fall" or "cast down" is "Napal" - it has a variety of meanings. Let me quote from the <u>Theological</u> <u>Wordbook</u> <u>of</u> <u>the</u> <u>Old</u> <u>Testament</u>, Harris, Archer, Waltke: "Besides the common physical action or occurrence, a violent or accidental circumstance is often indicated." In other words, sometimes the falling over is not planned or expected. I believe many times in the Bible God's people fell to the ground as a physical response to God's overwhelming manifest presence, which by the sheer power radiating from Him rendered human faculties senseless.

In Revelation we have an example of John falling over in the presence of Jesus; *"When I saw Him I fell at His feet as a dead man"* (Revelation 1:17). Both John's account here and Daniel's in Daniel 10:8-10 state they collapsed because, as dead men, they had no self-control left to themselves.

In the Garden of Gethsemane, the soldiers who had come to arrest Jesus drew back and fell to the ground when He identified Himself (John 18:6).

There are also scriptures that tell us people are thrown to the ground by demons when they manifest. If a mere demon can cause that reaction with some people, does it not stand to reason that the manifest presence of God can and would do much more, although the fruit obviously would be radically different (Mark 3:11, 9:20, Luke 8:28)!

Note: Many people have been the victims of well-meaning charismatic or Pentecostal ministers who have been heavy-handed. These people end up being pushed

j

by man rather than being overcome by the Spirit. Usually this is the result of over-zealousness on the part of those ministers who, because of poor role-modeling, carelessly (for the most part), feel they are helping God out. The main problem seems to be people and ministers who seek after an experience, rather than seeking after the Lord. These misguided ministers fail to allow God to do exactly what He wants, how He wants, and when He wants. Just as there are people who preach the gospel with false motives, you cannot throw out the baby with the bath water. There has never been a move of God, this side of heaven, that the flesh of man and counterfeit presence of the enemy has not been a least a little bit in evidence. We forget that even in Heaven itself there has been rebellion! So to claim that a move is not valid because there are some "flesh" and problems is in itself an invalid argument.

3) Weeping and Crying

We have noticed that one of the most common manifestations of the Holy Spirit's presence is weeping. Weeping has been a part of every revival that has occurred in the United States. Jonathan Edwards, D.L. Moody, and Charles Finney all spoke of people who were so overtaken by God that they broke down and wept.

I would remind the reader that countless people weep when they come to the altars of our churches every Sunday. Whether it is because of the pain they feel, the sin and guilt they carry, or the joy of knowing God has forgiven them and loves them, weeping is a regular experience of many at our worship services.

Scripture is full of passages that connect a humbling and repentant heart with weeping:

Joel 2:12,17   Judges 21:2,26
II Kings 22:19   Ezra 10:1
II Chronicles 34.27   Nehemiah 8:9

There are even passages of scripture where the Lord calls or commands His people to weep: *"In that day the Lord called you to weeping"* (Isaiah 22:12, Joel 2:1217, James 4:9).

In the Gospel of Luke Jesus call blessed those who weep (6:45).

In Nehemiah, we are told that the people wept when they heard the words of the law (Nehemiah 8:9).

There are examples of God's people weeping when they would come "before Him." *"And the people came to the house of God and abode there till evening before God, and lifted up their voices and wept"* (Judges 21:2). For further reading, see Judges 20:23, 21:26, and Luke 7:38.

Many times weeping is also an indication God is touching someone. The tears and grieving seem to heal a deep hurt or to minister love and forgiveness in a person's life. It is my belief that weeping occasionally can be part of the normative walk with God until we are with our Lord in heaven.

4) Stumbling, rocking back and forth, or "Drunk in the Spirit"

As Jeremiah prophesied concerning Judah, he said these words:

"I have become like a drunken man, even like a man overcome with wine because of the Lord and because of His word" (Jeremiah 23:9). It has been very common to see those who are filled with God's Spirit during this visitation try to preach, teach, or lead the meetings; they are overcome "like drunken men," unable to speak, walk, or stand.

On the day of Pentecost the Holy Spirit was poured out upon those early believers. They must have been acting like men and women drunk with wine, otherwise we would not have the following passage:

> Some, however, made fun of them and said, "They have had too much wine." Then Peter stood up with the Eleven, raised his voice and addressed the crowd: "Fellow Jews and all of you who live in Jerusalem, let me explain this to you; listen carefully to what I say. These men are not drunk, as you suppose. It's only nine in the morning! (Acts 2:13-15).

At numerous meetings I have looked around at how the Spirit of God was manifesting Himself on people and thought to myself, "If someone were to walk into this meeting not understanding what was happening, they would definitely think we had been drinking or had taken some sort of drug!" The manifestation of being "drunk in the Spirit" in the book of Acts is the same manifestation we are experiencing today. I, for one say, "Bless you Jesus for your works among us."

5) Laughing, the Joy of the Lord

As the holy Spirit has fallen upon people, many have begun to laugh uncontrollably and continue to laugh for some time. It has been very disconcerting for many to see (and hear) people laughing uncontrollably in church. But as I read through the Bible, I find many scriptures that speak of God's people being filled with joy, laughter, and gladness. We are told there should be joy and gladness in the presence of the Lord.

"They will be glad in Your presence"
(Isaiah 9:3)
"In Your presence is the fullness of Joy"
(Psalm 16:11).

*"You do make him joyful with gladness
in Your presence"* (Psalm 25:6).
*"The disciples were continually filled
with joy and the Holy Spirit"* (Acts 13:52).

What does it mean to be "continually filled with joy and the Holy Spirit?"

Is it really so far-fetched to believe that the disciples, as they were filled with the joy of the Lord, at times broke out in spontaneous and perhaps uncontrollable laughter?

What a far cry that must have been in comparison to our often dry, boring, overly somber services.

Speaking about those who would eventually come to know the Lord, Isaiah called them "foreigners." He prophesied, *"Even those I bring to My Holy mountain and make them joyful in my house of prayer"* (Isaiah 56:7). Isaiah also said, *"Joy and gladness will be found in her"* (Isaiah 51:3). "Her" refers to God's people as the bride of Christ.

Should we forget that Nehemiah told us "the joy of the Lord is our strength?" (Nehemiah 8:10), or that we have been *"anointed with the oil of gladness"* (Hebrews 1:9), and *"anointed with the oil of Joy"* (Psalm 45:7)?

Laughing may not be common in our churches in North America, but that is certainly nothing to brag about! If the Holy Spirit wants to fill an individual with "joy unspeakable," and it causes that person to laugh, then who are we to call that experience unholy, out of order, or not from the Lord?

Conclusion

In conclusion, there are those who would say about the five manifestations of the Holy Spirit discussed here, "I don't feel good about it, I don't have peace about all this, therefore it can't possibly be from God!" Perhaps these people should re-examine their reasoning, rather than basing their ultimate decision upon feelings. Let us remember the Bible says, *"The heart is more deceitful than all else and is desperately sick...who can understand it?"* (Jeremiah 17:9).

Many times people feel comfortable with the status quo and make judgments based solely on personal past experiences (or their lack thereof) and their predetermined spiritual biases. Since Adam and Eve, man has always felt more comfortable trying to intellectually understand God rather than seeking His face and allowing the God whose "thoughts are not your thoughts, neither are your ways my ways" to be God in our midst.

My friend, maybe your spiritual grid is wrong. Maybe there really is a spiritual and dynamic encounter with the Holy Spirit that you have never yet experienced. This view is a purely logical assumption, considering that God is so far above us and His ways are so far beyond our understanding (Isaiah 55:8-9).

Also, it is inadvisable to use as a measuring stick normal church activity to make judgments on the outpouring of God's Spirit. By its very definition a revival will result in unusual manifestations and activities.

From a pastoral perspective, the fruit of this outpouring has radically changed people and the whole spiritual atmosphere of our fellowship. Many have testified they have found a new love for and desire to follow our Lord Jesus. We have seen many repent and become Christians as a result of God's power encountering them at one of the meetings. Entire families have turned to the Lord! I truly believe the greatest determining factor of whether or not something is truly from God is the fruit it produces (John 15:4-8).

The fruit from this outpouring has surpassed our expectations, especially in the area of personal prayer, intercession, and daily devotions.

My prayer for our church and all who call upon the name of the Lord is this: "Come, Lord Jesus, fill us again, conform us to your image. Give us boldness to speak out in your name, that many may come to the true knowledge of our Savior Jesus Christ."

Appendix

A few verses demonstrating some of the effects of God's manifest presence

Exodus 33:14-15 - *"The LORD replied, 'My **Presence** will go with you, and I will give you rest.'"*

Leviticus 9:24 - *"Fire came out from the **presence** of the LORD and consumed the burnt offering and the fat portions on the altar. And when all the people saw it, they shouted for joy and fell, face down."*

Deut. 4:37 - *"Because he loved your forefathers and chose their descendants after them, he brought you out of Egypt by his **Presence** and his great strength."*

Deut. 12:7 - *"There, in the **presence** of the LORD your God, you and your families shall eat and shall rejoice in everything you have put your hand to, because the LORD your God has blessed you."*

I Samuel 6:20 - *"And the men of Beth Shemesh asked, 'Who can stand **in the presence** of the LORD, this holy God? To whom will the ark go up from here?"*

II Samuel 22:13 - *"Out of the brightness of his **presence** bolts of lightning blazed forth."*

II Kings 22:19 - *"'Because your heart was responsive and you humbled yourself before the LORD when you heard what I have spoken against this place and its people, that they would become accursed and laid waste, and because you tore your robes and **wept in my presence**, I have heard you,' declares the LORD."*

I Chron. 29:22 - *"They ate and drank with **great joy** in the **presence** of the LORD that day."*

II Chron. 34:27 - *"'Because your heart was responsive and you humbled yourself before God when you heard what he spoke against this place and its people, and because you **humbled** yourself before me and tore your robes and **wept** in my presence, I have heard you,' declares the LORD."*

Ezra 9:15 - *"O LORD, God of Israel, you are righteous! We are left this day as a remnant. Here we are before you in our guilt, though because of it not one of us can stand in your **presence**."*

Psalm 16:11 - *"You have made known to me the path of life; you will **fill me with joy** in your **presence**, with eternal pleasures at your right hand."*

Psalm 18:12 - *"Out of the brightness of his **presence** clouds advanced, with hailstones and bolts of lightning."*

Psalm 21:6 - *"Surely you have granted him eternal blessings and made him glad with the **joy of your presence**."*

Psalm 114:7 - *"**Tremble**, O earth, at the **presence** of the Lord, at the **presence** of the God of Jacob."*

Isaiah 26:17 - *"As a woman with child about to give birth writhes and cries out in her pain, so were we in your **presence**, O LORD."*

Jeremiah 5:22 - *"'Should you not fear me?' declares the LORD. 'Should you not **tremble** in my **presence**'?"*

Lamentations 2:19 - *"Arise, **cry** out in the night, as the watches of the night begin; **pour out your heart** like water in the **presence** of the Lord. **Lift up your hands** to him for the lives of your children, who faint from hunger at the head of every street."*

Ezekiel 38:20 - *"The fish of the sea, the birds of the air, the beasts of the field, every creature that moves along the ground, and all the people on the face of the earth will **tremble** at my **presence**. The mountains will be overturned, the cliffs will crumble and every wall will fall to the ground."*

Nahum 1:5 - *"The mountains quake before him and the hills melt away. The earth **trembles** at his **presence**, the world and all who live in it."*

Acts 2:28 - *"You have made known to me the paths of life; you will **fill me with joy in your presence**."*

I John 3:19 - *"This, then, is how we know that we belong to the truth, and how we set our hearts at **rest** in his **presence**."*